NOTEWORTHY NATURE

In and around Horsham town

Written by

Heather Glenny

Illustrated with her photographs and paintings

Grosvenor House
Publishing Limited

This book is published by
Grosvenor House Publishing Ltd
Link House
140 The Broadway, Tolworth, Surrey, KT6 7HT.
www.grosvenorhousepublishing.co.uk

A CIP record for this book
is available from the British Library

ISBN 978-1-80381-483-4

CONTENTS

AUTHOR'S NOTE

The information contained in this book is believed to be correct, though some errors may have occurred.

ACKNOWLEDGEMENTS

With thanks to Jacob Everitt for checking the labelling of names in this work and offering some very helpful comments on the text.

INTRODUCTION

My interest in nature was sparked from a young age, when I used to wander over the Surrey countryside near my home, noticing wild flowers, butterflies and birds. I would get home and look in books to find names and pictures of what I had seen and sometimes try to draw and paint them as well.

The concept and beginnings of writing this project were achieved several years before the Covid pandemic, when I was sifting through photographs and copious nature notes taken from 2004 until 2022 in the Horsham district. I have enjoyed relating some of these notes in this small book and hope that sharing this information may encourage others to explore the wildlife in their locality. It is in no way a comprehensive record of natural history, but just notes from observations I have made.

Many people have chosen nature as a subject for a book, especially during the lockdowns in 2020-21 and it's great that more of us should find natural history to be so fascinating and interesting. Nature is all around us whether in towns, villages or open spaces. Exploring your local area finding out about what grows or lives there can be most rewarding. Horsham has many green spaces all of these are likely to be host to many birds, flowers, insects and small animals.

Watching bird behaviour can be really interesting and it is good to question 'why is the bird behaving in that way?' It helps you learn more about how they live their lives. Particularly at the current time when wildlife from many green spaces is being squeezed out as the land is claimed for housing humans: you need to know what's out there before it disappears! Natural history is such a wide subject, where learning something new can be guaranteed and you'll never get bored observing the natural world around you. Taking photographs when you are out and about often helps with identification later, and a few scribbled notes are useful as well.

My approach in writing and using my own photographs to illustrate this book was to produce an uncomplicated and unscientific text to appeal to everyone as well as amateur naturalists. I have used common names rather than specific names wherever practical or possible.

CHAPTER ONE

MY HOME GARDEN 2003–2019

It was really fascinating to discover what actually lived in my own garden. It was amazing how many insects, birds and other wildlife liked to visit, lived in, or that shared my space. Watching them, and thinking about their behaviour, led to further understanding of what was on my own doorstep.

The size of the rear garden was 60 x 30 feet fenced all around, with a ten-foot conifer hedge at the bottom behind the rear boundary and fence line. At ground level, there was also a horseshoe-shaped gap in the easterly fence line for hedgehogs, foxes and maybe other wildlife to access my home patch. The aspect from the house was south-facing, getting sun for most of any sunny day, except in winter when the sun was so much lower in the sky. Then, a huge multi-trunked Conifer tree in a neighbour's plot tended to keep most of the garden in the shade and consequently it stayed damp when many winter storms blew in rather frequently. There was a small pond which was about one square metre in size. The soil was clay which was usual in this neighbourhood. As a keen gardener I created an herbaceous border and had a small number of shrubs. My preference was always to grow 'old-fashioned' simple flowers that would be more attractive for bees and other insects.

There were not a great many different species of birds on site since it was near to many other houses in a 1950's estate situation. Houses on the other side of my road backed on to some common land, known as Rookwood, with many trees, dense shrubs and two rivers providing some diverse habitats. The householders on that side saw many more bird species than could be expected in my garden.

Image 1 Setting the Scene: The rear garden in Summertime

When I moved to this property towards the end of 2003, there was no real garden at all, just unkempt grass and a couple of established Camellia bushes plus two dwarf Acers with twisted trunks that looked like oversized bonsai trees in winter. Additionally, there was a dilapidated old greenhouse centrally placed in the rear plot; quite an eyesore in fact – but it was a useful functional space to store some of my seedlings and tender plants at that time.

BIRDS

Every year I would note several pairs of House Sparrows, an unspecified number of Dunnocks, a pair of Blackbirds, Blue Tits, Great Tits, Coal Tits, Wrens, Robins, Greenfinches, Starlings, Collared Doves, Woodpigeons, many Jackdaws and Magpies in this garden. It was easy to imagine that I was living near the coast

Image 2   Many Herring Gulls on next door's roof – looking like they are watching a football match!

as there were often many noisy Herring Gulls, too. They have spread a lot further inland nowadays and seemed to enjoy the Horsham area where there was a local waste site, a local Nature Reserve as well as the Cootes Green pond, in my locality.

I have seen a few birds of prey around here and have witnessed a pair of Sparrowhawks – one of them grabbing a Starling for a snack. On another occasion they caught a Squirrel which they impaled on next door's apple tree before devouring the unfortunate animal. One afternoon I just happened to see a Sparrowhawk successfully ambush a Blackbird in the front garden immediately over the road. It tore its prey to bits and devoured it underneath the very bush where the Blackbird had been trying seek refuge. More recently Red Kites have been noticed high overhead as that species have extended their territories. There were frequent sightings of Buzzards, up to a dozen of them

Image 3 A Starling falls victim to the Sparrowhawk

sometimes, wheeling around at different times of the day high in the sky above the house.

Back in 2003 I often saw a Song Thrush or two on the lawn, and near the greenhouse there was a large stone they used as an anvil for breaking snail shells. Due to the damp clay conditions there were usually plenty of slugs and snails, but unfortunately, for a decade or so, I hadn't seen resident Thrushes in the garden. Though in winter I noticed occasional Thrushes on the lawn, but they would have been fleeting visitors dropping in to feast a bit and then carry on their journey. I often heard them in trees at Rookwood and other local places as well, but not as residents in my garden.

House Sparrows have been the most common birds I have seen during the time I was at this house. Several pairs have found places to nest around the soffits and front door porch each year. They drew attention to themselves daily by being very noisy in the Acer just outside my study window with almost incessant loud chirping and some rather typical squabbling. The collective term for Sparrows is a 'Quarrel of Sparrows' which I feel is very appropriate! Over the years I was really fortunate to see many of their fledglings. Unbelievably, a few have accidentally managed to get inside the house. I recall one day I heard some very strange fluttering and scraping noises from inside my electrical fuse and meter box in the hall, by the front door. To my surprise when I investigated inside the box, I found a sparrow fledgling had fallen down the exposed cavity wall and was stuck in there. I managed to free it and put it outside the front door below the nest site.

Image 4 The Sparrow in the conservatory, having a wonderful time in the dust bath!

Within a few moments the mother had it perched on the Acer where she fed it and very soon it was able to fly well enough to be with the rest of its family. On another occasion, and I confess this incident lasted for two whole days, I went around from room to room because I could hear some loud chirping, but could not locate exactly where it was coming from. I realised it must be another fledgling. Eventually I discovered the small bird behind a wooden chest but I'll never know how it managed to be there. As it was at the rear of the house, I carefully cupped it in my hand and placed it on an old Lavender bush near the back door. I thought it might be too dangerous at ground level since other people's cats strolled into my garden occasionally. Within a very short space of time – no more than ten minutes – the mother bird heard the youngster's chirps and was reunited with her errant offspring.

One hot summer's day I left my conservatory double doors open for good ventilation whilst I went off to do some shopping. At the end of the day when I closed the doors for the night, I suddenly realised I was not alone in there. Having a lovely dust bath in the earth of my Strelitzia plant tub was an adult sparrow and when it had finished bathing it perched on a leaf stalk of the shrub as though settling down for the night. I had to re-open the doors again to gently usher it outside. In spring 2014, I was amused to see several very young sparrows perched in a row on the top of a trellis and Escallonia hedge near where the bird feeders were situated (so there was adequate cover for birds in case of any predators) and the parent sparrows were teaching them how to get food from the feeders by taking a tiny bit to each little bird in turn. Much later on that same day these House Sparrow fledglings were clinging on to the bird feeders. At one point there were nine little sparrows fluttering and flapping about rather clumsily on the seed feeder and the fat balls.

At the bottom of the garden on some old greenhouse staging I used to leave a large shallow seed tray filled with water throughout the summer. One day I heard quite a chirpy commotion coming from the far end of the garden where there is an adjacent apple tree. Several House Sparrows were taking turns to fly down for a bath and splash about in the tray before returning to their perch to preen and dry off. I observed they were often there at a similar time of day in the early afternoon. Observing the behaviour of these birds has been delightful and very rewarding. Sparrows tend to live their lives staying close to the same place, except for a period in August where they leave to feast on an abundance of seeds in fields within a mile or so from 'home'.

Dunnocks were formerly known as Hedge Sparrows and they scurry about the ground and low spaces, often picking up crumbs dropped from the bird feeders in the rear garden. It might be thought they lead dull lives as they are drab-looking little brown and grey birds but in fact, studies of their behaviour have uncovered some big surprises. They have been more closely observed in recent years and we now know much more about them. In fact, they are up to no good for much of the time. They are rather promiscuous birds and are unfaithful to their partners. The female allows a male to mate with her but then she mates with other males invited into her territory. The new male pecks at her vent area to remove the previously deposited sperm before he mates with her. I have actually witnessed this behaviour away from the bird feeders, behind the Escallonia hedge. This 'free love' strategy is thought to be so that the best genes are invested in the next generation and quite importantly, several males help to feed the young who then have a really good chance of survival. As this behaviour has definitely occurred in my garden, I can't be certain how many Dunnocks there could have been in my own patch, but I noticed their presence most days of the year. A while ago, I was concerned when a neighbour cut down and grubbed out a fence line row of shrubs in which I was fairly sure some Dunnocks were nesting. Nesting birds should NOT be disturbed and householders should always check to make sure no birds are nesting before cutting down hedges and trees in springtime and early summer. A while later, I saw some Dunnocks back under the bird feeders, though I suspect a new nest had now been built somewhere else.

I really enjoy the Dunnock's regular song which is a pretty, tuneful ditty with a sudden end; as though somehow the ending is cut off. They seemed quite tame, never bothering when I was pottering about in the garden.

I loved to see a pair Blackbirds choosing to nest here but often the outcome of their raising a family would usually end badly, because Magpies cunningly time their nest attacks to steal the nestlings when they are just a few days old in order to feed themselves or their own young. However, the pair of Blackbirds never seemed to give up and after a couple of days of recuperation and mourning, they returned to build a new nest in a different bush or maybe in the conifer hedge. A new nest took a few days to complete and I have watched the nest building activity on several occasions. The female began with grasses and very thin twigs followed by a wet mud lining, and finally some dry grasses or moss for comfort and cosiness for the eggs. I have also witnessed them coupling on my summerhouse roof, after which new eggs are laid and duly hatched. Sadly, this whole process was repeated with up to three new nests in a season and the Magpies always watched of all the activity and timed their raids. The huge Conifer tree that towered over three or four gardens provided the Magpies with a reliable high perch from which they staked out where they could strike for their next meal.

Fortunately, I have had some happier encounters with the Blackbirds over the years. One year a female became quite tame when I threw a handful of mealworms out by the backdoor and she would immediately appear and eat them right in front of me. Sometimes if I had forgotten to do this, when I went into the kitchen there she was waiting by the door. She'd stand there for a long time, until I opened the door slowly and quietly to put the mealworms out. On another occasion during an extremely hot spell of weather when the Blackbird was nest building, she was having difficulty finding any wet mud with which to line her nest. She found me planting out some small plants in my border and as I watered them in, she flew down really close, brushing my hand

Image 5 The not-so-timid female Blackbird enjoying some mealworms outside the backdoor in October 2005

as she did so and took a beak full of wet mud back to the nest. A process she repeated several times that same day so I emptied the watering can out on a bare patch of soil in case she might need some more wet soil.

Several years back in the middle of March, the Blackbirds had been foraging in the garden every day for two weeks and I couldn't help wondering if they are the same pair that tried to have three broods in the previous year. Watching them one morning I witnessed a small drama take place. I noticed two female Blackbirds keeping a distance from one another and a male Blackbird plus another male that had just appeared in the garden. The latter was promptly seen off by the first male in spectacular fashion. They were spiralling up together, talons outstretched about two metres above ground level. This sparring had me

9

completely transfixed and it went on for about twenty minutes, after which, the original female emerged from the undergrowth and the male resident bird settled back into the garden. This event was something so interesting to watch yet could so easily have been missed if I hadn't made a point of observing in the garden regularly. As it happens, very recently a second male Blackbird again entered the garden and had daily confrontations and has had fights with the resident one on four consecutive days, but the intruder finally left the territory. Unfortunately, I have never been able to capture this behaviour on camera though it would have made a superb home video.

In mid-summer some time ago, after the Blackbird pair spent three days building a nest in a Kiwi-fruit bush against the fence, some days later the first chick hatched. I had concerns about the chances of a successful brood so late at this site. About 5 a.m. the next day I was awakened to a terrible din. The male Blackbird was valiantly trying to ward off yet another Magpie attack. Sadly, the Magpie was again the victor. The male Blackbird was quite dishevelled and some feathers on his right wing were somewhat out of place. Unbelievably, despite all these events, the Blackbirds began nest building yet again a bit further along in the same bush. I was anxious for them as I am sure the Magpies have already noticed them from the Conifer tree.

Gardening near my greenhouse one day the female Blackbird was foraging very close by. She espied a bumblebee walking in some clover in the uncut lawn and she rushed past me to snatch it at ground level. To my surprise, she then pecked the bee several times before swallowing it completely.

An unusually stupid Woodpigeon has been trying to build a nest of loose sticks above my rose arch. Thankfully after an hour or two, it seemed to lose interest and didn't bother to finish it. Maybe it was just practising. This was just as well because after a few windy days all the twigs fell to the ground.

Around early April the garden was always full of birdsong and activity. My attention was drawn daily to the never-changing song of a Dunnock merrily singing on the fence line shrubs. Three pairs of House Sparrows raided the garden feeders throughout the day mostly on the peanuts or seed mix feeders. Other birds visiting were Blue Tits and Great Tits, Jackdaws including 'Odd-bod', a mixed-plumage young bird who tried to cling on to the fat-ball feeder, plus two Collared Doves, and several Magpies were also in the garden. The male Blackbird was still defending his territory fervently from any other Blackbirds and I couldn't help wondering if they ever noticed the Magpies constructing a nest near the top of the neighbouring huge Conifer tree. Unusually in my own garden at this time, I heard a Chiffchaff and a Nuthatch but I did not see either of them, but their songs and the Nuthatch's alarm call are very distinctive.

I need to say more about the bird I have named 'Odd-bod'. It was in 2010, and this bird was always amongst all the Jackdaws visiting the garden and he perched often on the westerly fence. He was then like a fattish blackbird-size and had many white and speckled feathers. At first, I considered he might have been a part-albino blackbird, but later as he grew up and was seen again the following year, I concluded he was an odd Jackdaw that had a partial magpie appearance – hence the name I gave him. His breast and flanks were white with black specks and his head and nape were grey, but on his back in a U-shape he had white feathers, but his wings were dark. He had a Jackdaw's tail feathers as they were not long like a Magpie's. He was always totally accepted by his Jackdaw companions.

I categorised all local Jackdaws as 'a bit of a nuisance' but this was because they pecked and pulled out any new plants in the front garden. They also tore away the felt layer on the shed roof and on the flat roof over the dormer window, eventually rendering them both non-waterproof, thus incurring expense on my part for repairs. I saw 'Odd-bod ' the next year too, but not after that. He would have been mature enough to breed so he may have moved

Image 6   Odd-bod on the left, a Magpie and a Jackdaw

out to another territory. Jackdaws usually live about three years or sometimes more.

In 2013 there were many Greenfinches in and around the garden mostly perched on any higher trees nearby and singing their distinctive song. By 2015 although there was only the occasional Greenfinch around as the numbers were much decreased from those experienced previously. The fall in numbers may well have been due to a disease called *Trichomonosis* which has been prevalent in recent years from about 2005, I believe.

Around June time there were three newly-fledged Blue Tits sitting in a row on the rose arch near the bird feeders. The parent birds went mad with alarm calls as I walked by to open the greenhouse doors, but the babes just sat there not knowing what the fuss was about. The parents were picking bits of fat out of the feeder and

Image 7   Old and young Starlings feeding on the lawn. Photo taken at the end of May 2015

taking it to each of the little ones in turn. I presumed they were showing them that the bird feeders were another good source of food when required, though I guessed that within a week or so the little ones would be finding seeds or insects for themselves and would be independent young birds.

One day I returned home to find a fledging Great Tit on my front doorstep. I did not disturb it and it was gone soon afterwards, so I hoped it was reunited with its parents.

Sometimes there were many Starlings on the grass verges outside the bungalow, but occasionally I saw quite a few in the back garden. Depending on the time of year, there could be a mix of young and older Starlings. Sometimes people do not recognise the pale brown birds as young starlings because the adults have dark, iridescent feathers.

FLOWERS

Writing up my scribbled nature notes which spanned several previous years, I have realised how different weather conditions and temperatures have affected the dates for sightings of birds, plants, insects and so on. 2016 started in a particularly mild way following on from the mildest autumn/winter ever recorded. January was unusually wet, too. The mild temperatures seemed to have confused many plants into bloom that normally were not open till late February or March. For instance, on Christmas Day 2015 there were several plants in my own garden that were in flower, these were: an unknown species of Clematis with white bell-like flowers, a strong-scented Daphne shrub was already flowering, a Daffodil was in bloom in the front garden, some double Anemones, an everlasting Wallflower ('Bowles Mauve'), some small yellow, scented Wallflowers, Polyanthus, small Cyclamens, Winter Jasmine and some mauve Heather. All these were flowering weeks earlier than usual. The climate also affects other aspects of natural history. There were one or two very large bumblebees about, and a few other early bees and insects flying around as well. Some overwintering butterflies had also been tricked into waking up too soon but it is probable they may have perished in the colder conditions that followed in February. There were some Sparrows in the garden on or around the feeders but also a Robin, Dunnock, Blackbirds, Blue Tits, Great Tits and a Coal Tit were all present, as well as a few Magpies, Jackdaws and Woodpigeons. I also saw a pair of the more delicate-looking Collared Doves on the apple tree.

The only wild flower actually blooming out of season at the turn of the year, 2015 into 2016, was the Red Campion. Each year I always allowed clumps of these self-set 'weeds' to flourish in the herbaceous border as they added colour and height and also flower for many months. In the wilder shaded area at the end of the garden there were some Teasels flowering and if word gets round, maybe Goldfinches might come for the seeds later on. Arum Lilies also grew there producing scarlet berries late in the autumn. In this area I grew Foxgloves, Mullein, St. John's Wort, Lungwort, Woodruff and some

Evening Primroses. Wild shrubby roses with very small red hips grew there too as many years ago, I found some rose hips in my pocket on returning from a camping holiday. I potted them up and they grew into to sizeable plants so I put them in this unkempt area. Around the same area was a natural clump of Honesty that developed on its own over a few years. I really enjoyed seeing the simple mauve flowers and later on the fascinating 'penny' seed pods, which are papery and almost transparent in texture so you can see all the seeds around the edge of the case. The Honesty added a large clump of purple colour where little else blooms in the spring. I had Valerian growing wildly in my front garden but I frequently pulled some of it out so it didn't spread everywhere. Additionally, in the front lawn I occasionally discovered some small Cowslips, tiny Violas, and some Violets growing. Cowslips also grew in the grass verge by the road.

Plants flowering in February included Snowdrops, tiny Cyclamen, Crocus, Daffodils, and the sweet-smelling Daphne still had a few flowers. The yellow-flowered Winter Jasmine has all but finished by this time. In the last two weeks I had the opportunity to get gardening after a spell of really wet weather. A few sessions of activity enabled me to sort out part of the front garden, prune my Wisteria and both Grapevines. I left the Roses over the arch for the time being. My lawns got their first cut of the year even though they were still very soggy, as the mild conditions enabled the grass to grow taller every day, so a rough cut was essential before it was too long for my small underpowered mower.

Early in the year has always been the time to plan what plants would be needed once the weather warmed up, and I considered plants that would attract bees and other insects, plus some extra plants that I had not tried for a few years. I have always preferred the simpler plants but have never liked complicated sterile hybrids that served no purpose for insects. Cultivated perennial plants I grew in my border included: Inula, Penstemons, Geums, Geraniums, the Pineapple Plant, old-fashioned Shasta Daisies, Hollyhocks, Phlox, perennial Wallflowers a standard Bay tree, Hibiscus, and some Roses.

INSECTS

Of course, there would be hundreds of undiscovered insects in the garden but the more I looked, the more I'd find! I was always pleased to see different types of bees here. There were a good number of bumblebees noticeable from January to almost the end of the year. In fact, in mid-December 2016 I saw a huge bumblebee buzzing loudly outside the conservatory. I still find it difficult to be sure about accurately identifying bees, though I am now working on this! Many of the bumblebees I noticed had buff or silver tails and some had red tails. I also had Leaf-cutter Bees and the Common Carder Bumblebees on site. When the Lungwort flowered the Bee-fly, which has a very long proboscis, was quick to feed on the blue and pink small flowers.

In the first week of April in 2010 a beautiful and pristine Peacock Butterfly was resting on a patch of sunlit soil, warming up – maybe it had come out of the shed that I opened up earlier that day. Within five minutes it was off, sampling nectar from a nearby Hyacinth, after which it flew over the garden fence. There were two very large bumble bees looking for flowers to settle on and one visited the Flowering Currant shrub. Today the dark red Camellia flowers have joined the spring floral bonanza which comprised Daffodils, Narcissus, Polyanthus, Lungwort, Cowslips, Heathers, Flowering Currant, Forsythia, and the last few Daphne fragrant flowers. In a damp area near the pond there were some Cuckoo flowers and Garlic Mustard – the favoured food-plants of Orange-tip caterpillars. I enjoyed watching Orange-tip Butterflies warming themselves in a sunny spot. The female Orange-tip is of course, duller in appearance without the flash of orange, but I have noticed them around the pond area. A few years ago, 2009 I think, we had a really hot summer and there was a major migration of Painted Lady Butterflies that turned up in the South of England. I was delighted to witness many of them visiting my Valerian as they made way further north. Theirs is an interesting migration because it is over such a distance, and several countries, that it takes more than one generation to accomplish the journey. This means that the Painted Ladies that arrive here, may have been caterpillars in Spain or somewhere and those that originated the journey have long since perished after laying their eggs en route, so the life-cycle would be continued.

A 'star turn' in the insect life has to be the Hummingbird Hawk-moth that visited my Valerian a few summers ago in September. I was so mesmerised that I watched it for some time before my brain engaged to go and get my camera and record it! Some weeks before, in early August, I had found a large green caterpillar on a shrubby red Salvia bush and after checking in a book realised this was the Hummingbird Hawk-moth caterpillar. I would mention that during 2022, I was able to see these Hawk-

Image 8 Knot Grass caterpillar

moths flying again in several different locations. On a summer's day in my pond area, with Iris stems sticking up out of the water, I once discovered a colourful caterpillar with spiky, hairy tufts red and pale markings on all segments climbing near the top of a stem.

It was later identified as a Knot Grass caterpillar that feeds on docks, brambles, plantains and herbaceous plants. The double-brooded moths appear in May or August.

Once, I also found the empty case of a dragonfly nymph three-quarters of the way up an Iris stem. This happens when they emerge at night time after spending about two years in the pond for their brief life as an adult.

I often looked around the garden to see what insects I could find amongst the greenery. Ladybird species which have also been confusing to identify. Most of the ones I have seen here are orange-red with black spots, but some had cream-spots. It is even more difficult now that the native ones have been rather outgunned by the invading Harlequin species. I have found the 2-spot Ladybird,

Image 9   Hummingbird Hawk-moth on Valerian (in the centre of picture) September 2013

which has different forms, one of which is black with red spots, which in my opinion, is similar in appearance to one of the non-native Harlequin Beetles. Also found were 7-spot Ladybirds and the 10-spot which is also variable in its form. I've quite often seen a 22-spot bright yellow Ladybird, which feeds on mildews rather than aphids. Several forms of the Harlequin Ladybirds have been noticed, and I have also found Harlequin larvae on my rose arch. 'Normal' looking ladybirds with lots of spots are also, I believe, Harlequins. To learn more, I have just ordered a field guide on Ladybirds and their larvae. Hopefully, I will be able to sort them out in future, as I have realised you can't just count up the spots in order to identify them!

Bee-flies have been buzzing all around the springtime Lungwort flowers, making a high-pitched buzz, which is different from a bee's buzz. I have found them fascinating to watch with their long

Image 10 Red-tailed Bumblebee on an Evening Primrose flower

Image 11 White-tailed Bumblebee on a Geum flower

proboscis as they busily collect the nectar. Other insects attracted to the Lungwort flowers are Common Carder Bumblebees, which have a block of gingery hair on their backs. Early in June I wandered around my garden taking photos of any bees on different flowers. I was curious to know if certain shaped flowers attracted particular types of bees. Some bees would rob the flower of nectar by making a hole near to the nectar when they could not enter the flower normally – perhaps because the flower was not flat and open to land on, but had a trumpet elongated shape. I realised later that most of the bees in the garden were either Buff-tailed or White-tailed Bumblebees, and there were also less often, Red-tailed Bumblebees. I also saw a bee-like insect that was almost totally black but I haven't been able to identify it. At the time there seemed to be fewer Honeybees about than in other years.

Before leaving the subject of bees, in mid-summer I discovered a Leaf-cutter Bee in the garden that has made a nest in a cavity underneath an old sink trough full of dwarf plants. I first noticed semi-circular holes with clean edges in the middle of my Strelitzia leaves when the plant was outside for the summer. I watched out for the culprit and eventually I saw the Leaf-cutter Bee taking a piece of leaf back to the trough, where it entered through a hole underneath. They are Solitary Bees that line their nest with the 'pushed in' leaves and fill them with nectar and pollen and then lay an egg on each leaf. Leaf-cutter Bees collect pollen under their abdomen and not on their hind legs like other bees.

Image 12 Cockchafer Beetle. Photo in May 2017

I have found different types of Shield Bug in the garden. One was identified as a Sloe Shield Bug, sometimes called Hairy Shield Bug, and that was on a large Geranium clump. A Forest Shield Bug, was found in the front garden in late summertime wandering along an external windowsill. Adults feed on insects and fruit, but larvae feed on deciduous trees in their usual habitat of woodland and gardens. One day, whilst working near my roses, I heard a whirring noise and so turned and looked up to find a Cockchafer Beetle, on the rose arch. It was a metallic copper and green beetle that flies from May to October, and feeds on rose flowers. The chubby larvae though feed on decaying leaves, plants and roots. It pupates in the soil or rotten wood over winter and emerges as an adult in spring. Their life cycle takes two years to complete.

Another species I noticed more recently was the Western Conifer Seed Bug, with its long antennae climbing up the window of my summerhouse. This bug is a fairly recent

Image 13 Western Conifer Seed Bug on the summerhouse glass. Photo October 2016

'invader' to Britain that is being monitored for the amount of damage it may be causing as it feeds on Pine. It is native to North America.

Just outside my back door I came across an Angle Shades Moth, camouflaged on the fence panel which was covered with evergreen Honeysuckle.

Unusually this moth had a red form but they are more often seen in a green form. These moths can be found at any time of year and use a wide variety of food plants. I am currently interested in looking for more moth species that inhabit my garden, but of course since they are mostly nocturnal that will be a work-in-progress for the future.

A very small moth that has beautiful crimson and gold colouring was a delight to find in my garden. I only recently found this here at home, but have written more about this small moth which I also discovered some years ago in the Horsham Museum Garden. (see Mint Moth, Chapter 2).

The largest of the UK Beetles is the Stag Beetle, which is good to see in the garden since they are now less common generally. The male is large with huge jaws and the females look much more a stubby, rounded shape without the antler-like jaws. They might

Image 14   Angle Shades Moth – Red Form. Photo taken late March 2015

feed on sap oozing from trees, but it is not really known if the adults do eat. The female lays eggs which hatch into white larva with a brown head, and which will live underground below deadwood (which they consume) for about five years before pupating. The whole life cycle takes up to seven years.

Of course, there are other insects that are not very welcome such as Froghoppers (Common Spittle-bugs) bringing disease to roses, but we often find its nymph's cuckoo-spit all around plant growth. The larvae are protected inside the frothy spit and feed by sucking sap from the food plant.

An unwelcome Micro-moth I have had doing its life-cycle in my conservatory is from the Tortrix Moth family, a small Fruit-tree Moth. This came in because my three Citrus shrubs were outside during the summer months and brought into the conservatory for the winter, usually at the end of September before any frosts. Lots of caterpillar frass collected around various conservatory plants and there were holes in some Citrus leaves. A few days later, some leaves were stuck together or rolled up until finally, the hatchings of quite a few of these little moths emerged from the pipe-like hard pupa cases. The very small caterpillars of this pest are grey-green.

FAUNA

This includes Toads, Frogs, Newts, Grass Snakes, Hedgehogs, Foxes, a Wood Mouse, and a tiny, Common Shrew which have all been seen in the garden. I am also including Spiders, Slugs and Snails here, too.

Having a fairly small pond of approximately one square metre is still big enough for wildlife to flourish. We didn't have a particularly good summer in 2015 as much of it was cold and damp, but when we had an early spell of very hot weather in late April, I espied a Grass Snake curled up in undergrowth on the northern edge of the pond. That is only the second time I have seen one in my own home patch. I know Grass Snakes are harmless to humans, but I prefer not to get too close. Every year, there were several small Frogs in the pond and they often used to just poke their heads up through the surface of the water, between the oxygenating plants. This happened so regularly that my youngest grandchild used to identify me as "Nana Frog"! However, I got caught out once by noticing a pointed snout in the pond and bent down pointing at it. I withdrew my hand very quickly when I suddenly realised it was actually the tip a Grass Snake's head and the rest of it was coiled on the edge of the pond. There have always been a good number of Common Newts in the pond too, and they feed on tadpoles and dragonfly larvae, plus other very tiny creatures. Newts were apparent in the pond about March time, but in the late summer they left the pond to hide under small rocks and then eat things like worms, slugs and snails during the winter. The young newt larvae develop their front legs first, which is different from the way tadpoles develop. Newts can live to about ten years. I think they are an attractive addition to our limited wildlife as they move gracefully in the water and the males have orange-spotted bellies in the breeding season.

When I first moved in here, someone local said *'Oh yes, that's the house with the hedgehogs in the garden'*. I deliberately left a reasonable-sized hole at the base of my easterly fence to allow Hedgehogs (and Red Foxes apparently) a means of entering or exiting my otherwise contained garden space. Hedgehogs are not often seen during the day since they are night foragers but one year, when glancing out of my kitchen window I saw a Hedgehog just outside. It was snuffling around but it soon scurried off on catching sight of my silhouette at the window. It can be an ominous sign to see them out in daylight, especially if they are young and underweight at the time when hibernation is appropriate. The very mild conditions at the end of 2015 may have inappropriately confused some hibernating animals into activity instead of sleep.

In 2003, before I decided to demolish my rickety old garage, just behind the rear wall in the undergrowth, I came across a tiny

Common Shrew. I cupped it in my hand to take a closer look as I had never really seen one so close before. It was such a lovely little creature, much smaller than I had imagined. It had dark brown silky fur that was paler underneath, and very small eyes. I replaced it where I had found it. Shrews are most active at night, have a good sense of smell and since they do not hibernate, they have to find food all year round.

I have seen several different species of Spider here at home. One summer I found an amazing hatching of hundreds of buff-coloured Garden-spiderlings with their black 'triangles' on their backs, as well the webbing they were emerging from.

After I had been scrambling around weeding and tidying amongst the shrubs and perennials in my border, I went indoors and discovered that clinging to my trouser leg was a beautiful yellow spider. I later identified it as a female Crab Spider which apparently

Image 15 The spiderlings emerging from the web in June 2015

sits on flower heads matching her body colour (which she can change), in order to prey on insects that land on the flower, relying on ambush, so this spider does not need to spin a web to catch its prey. Unfortunately, I discovered later on that my photograph of this lovely-coloured spider was totally blurred and unusable so it had to be deleted. There are many common garden spiders but some we notice more by their webs on dewy autumn mornings like the Garden Spider for instance. This is an orb weaver and the female is larger than the male and sits within the orb waiting to catch her meal. She has some white markings in the form of a cross on her abdomen. Also, the autumn denotes the start of their mating season. What I find fascinating is looking for different types of spider webs. There's the orb type, funnel type and some that look like a tangled mess but all are very successful in ensnaring prey. The cobweb thread is an amazingly strong material, and the webs show up so much more in the autumn, when the dew highlights the threads like rows of delicate pearls.

Jumping Spiders also live here, they have great eyesight. They have eight eyes spread around with some at the back and two larger eyes at the front. They rarely spin webs as they tend to jump on their prey. One that I have seen is the Zebra Spider, in their smart striped 'zebra-like' bodies, they stalk prey on walls.

Slugs and Snails are plentiful here, but they often devour my long-tended seedling plants after I have just planted them out. It has always upset me that I have nurtured the seedlings for over six weeks, planted them out and then overnight they are lost to the slugs and snails. There are several different types of snail, should you ever stop to seek them out: but I think the snail we see with a brown and yellow shell is more attractive than the dull Common Snail and I believe they do less damage to plants than the common ones. Frogs, Toads and Hedgehogs do consume some of course, but it depends on the numbers of the pests whether or not to intervene with any type of slug killer method. I have preferred not to do put poison pellets out, as I don't want to harm other creatures, particularly birds. The Song Thrush would have helped

Image 16   The Hedgehog near the conservatory. Photo taken June 2011

by eating snails and slugs, too, but sadly has not recently been seen in the garden, except for a few fleeting visitors in the early winter months.

There was a Red Fox, who regularly used my garden as part of its nightly wanderings. Usually at about 9.30pm it would come across the road from the Rookwood area, up my drive and over my side gate, or sometimes over the summerhouse, to the rear garden. If nothing interested him here, he would go over the fence at the bottom of the garden and on to wherever his night trail took him. One sunny day though I saw a shape curled up and totally relaxed just outside my greenhouse. When I glanced down the path, I imagined for a split-second that it was an apparition of my old dog come to visit my garden, but of course, it was a fox. Having seen this fox in daylight I observed that it had a lovely shiny coat looked well fed and very healthy.

Foxes may disturb people in the dead of night with their piercing autumnal screams during their mating season. The young are born in early springtime. Foxes are omnivores and so eat a varied diet which includes duck, rodents, earthworms, and scraps of food discarded by humans. They are notorious for their ability to easily tear bags of waste and extract anything that can keep them fed when nature's food is scarce.

A fox story I must relate is that in 2018/2019 a wonderful, exciting series of events regarding foxes was to unfold in my garden and lead to a fox family den immediately next door. The wise fox made the den there because the house had been empty for two years following the death of my neighbour, and the garden was unattended throughout that time. So, the fox, ever an opportunist, made its home behind the shed there with no human disturbance. The situation leading up to this was when I had noticed a mature fox preening and resting till nightfall in the last week of August 2018. In early September I saw that there were two adult foxes resting up during the day next door. Thereafter to the end of 2018, one of them was sometimes there if weather was fine, but not on rainy days.

On 24th January 2019 both adult foxes were around in the morning. The first was there at 9 a.m. but an hour later I witnessed and photographed the other fox (with white edges to the ears and a white patch at the end of its tail) in my garden sniffing the air as it could detect that the second fox was next door. Suddenly it jumped over the fence and there was a very 'noisy' encounter! They then went on a chase over several back gardens, still making plenty of noise for quite a while.

During April I noticed that the fox-track through my garden was still being used, though I did not actually see a fox until the last week of April.

What joy though when I looked out at dusk on 6th May to see the vixen (with blacker markings and a black end to the tail) feeding

Image 17   A Fox just sitting around, near to the neighbouring fence in January 2019

and playing with four small cubs in next door's garden. One of them was very overexcited and it had a white tip to its tail; it was so unruly that the vixen had to sometimes collect it up in her mouth and move it back with the other three. I watched them discreetly from my upstairs window for a while until the daylight was fading into darkness. During the next few weeks, I enjoyed watching the cubs at play next door, fighting and chasing in a delightful way. They were growing quickly so they must be fed well by the parents. Then, because the vixen had joined in with finding prey for them, the cubs were left on their own in the garden next door. They were not at that time capable of jumping the fence between the gardens, but there was also a gap under my westerly fence that had been scraped out and so, the two most inquisitive and adventurous cubs found they could squeeze through. I was in my conservatory and on glancing out, saw the cubs exploring everything in my garden. I was lucky enough to take some short videos on my camera as they didn't seem to have noticed me and the recordings are a precious 'keepsake' now.

Image 18 The Fox and four young cubs in next door's overgrown garden in May 2019

They played with items they found and knocked over some flowerpots. Then they seemed fascinated by watching the bees on some flowers. One ran out under my side gate into the drive and looked across the road, the other ran back to the safety of next door's garden. Somehow the one that ran out came back safely later, though I am not sure if the vixen came back that way when returning to the den, or if it found its own way back.

It was so lovely to watch these cubs grow and play until they were nearly as large as the adults. In the middle of August, I noted that both adults and just one cub was next door. Inevitably, the time comes for the families to split up and the young ones are sent off to fend for themselves and live elsewhere. By the 18th August there was just one young one resting next door, and then none were seen at all for several weeks until a very wet day when I noticed two foxes curled up underneath the hedge. After that, no sightings at all.

Another mammal in my garden was a Wood Mouse. It was a non-bird-like movement that attracted my attention below the bird feeders and I quickly realised it was a mouse. It was carefully and methodically climbing up the shrubby Magnolia in order to get some free bird food bounty. I found it very amusing to watch because, from the base it would climb as high as it could until its own weight bent the narrow twigs away from the food, so it went down to the ground and started again climbing up another small branch with the same result. It did this many times before finally giving up. A few months later on, I opened my wooden 'wellies' box near my backdoor as I thought I'd left my gardening gloves in there. Shock horror! There staring back at me with twinkling eyes, was a very beautiful Wood Mouse sitting all nice and cosy in my best walking boots. It had built a very comfy looking nest. After it had dashed past me, I reluctantly placed my walking boots into my dustbin! However, I was pleased to find it hadn't nested in or

Image 19 The little Wood Mouse is in the centre of the picture in the Magnolia

messed up my wellingtons which had been next to the walking boots. Was it the same mouse that I had seen climbing up my Magnolia in mid-April, I wondered? Wood Mice are distinctive as they have large ears, a yellowish brown back and a long tail. They are usually nocturnal creatures. The one I saw in April must have been very hungry to be foraging in the daytime.

FUNGI, LICHENS AND MOSSES

Of course, it is not always good when fungi are found in a cultivated garden as they maybe most unwelcome, as for example, Honey Fungus, or Mildews. The Roses do suffer most years with Mildew when the weather is too hot and dry, and with Black Spot as well. I also found some really small fungi growing up through the front lawn (which was also very mossy) and usually quite damp. In autumn these are very common and could be Fairy-Ring Fungus, but if there are only one or two similar looking fungi they could possibly be Brown Mottlegills, but I am not sure of the correct names. This is another area of natural history I need to learn more about.

Lichens are notoriously difficult to name correctly but I am always interested to see them on woody plants and trees, as it usually suggests good air quality as they don't live in polluted places. Lichens are neither plants nor animals. They are composite organisms arising from Algae and sometimes exist with Fungi. Grey-green crusty scales or tufts attach to twigs or branches. They make their own food from air and water and so are not parasitic. It is good to note various grey-green types, sometimes in partnership with a small fungi, as well as the orange/yellow types you might see on stones. Pixie Cup Lichen, half-algae and half-fungus, takes the form of tiny cups on a raised stem and it is the fungal element that fruits at the tips which are a scarlet red colour and lives on a species of moss. Mosses are also another species difficult to identify as there are more variations than might be supposed. I haven't yet tried to identify any of them, but I enjoy seeing them on tree trunks and roots or covering stones and rocks. There seem to be few books available on Mosses.

Images 20 & 21 Above: Example of Mosses and Lichen growing together on logs. Below: examples of different Lichens growing on a tree trunk. (Neither example is from my own garden)

CHAPTER TWO
THE HORSHAM
MUSEUM GARDEN

I have been involved with the maintenance of this beautiful garden since February 2004 when I volunteered to lead a small team of gardeners to keep it looking good throughout the years and for the public to enjoy. During the nineteen years (and still counting) of doing so I have noted a considerable amount of wildlife that visit or live in it. This delightful walled garden evokes an air of calmness whenever time is spent there. Some Horsham residents

Image 22 Overall view of the Museum Garden (taken in July 2005)

might be surprised to know of its existence, but it has always been open to all whenever the Museum is open. It contains many herbs and plants from times gone by. One bed contains mostly culinary herbs, another has household and strewing plants, the third bed has medicinal plants, and the fourth bed is full of fragrance when the Myrtle blooms. There are some very old roses such as the two Gallica Roses and there's a Bourbon Rose, a Moss Rose, Portland Rose and some special climbers all with lovely strong scents. The herbs are quite pungent, too, especially the Lemon Verbena, Myrtle, Bay and Rosemary. This garden happens to be roughly the same size as the garden in the previous chapter; that is about 60 x 30 feet.

BIRDS

Most of the time, there seemed to be a pair of Blackbirds, Blue Tits, a Robin and Woodpigeons foraging in the garden and some of them have nested there. Certainly, the Blackbirds and Blue Tits have nested for several years in the upper reaches of the climbing roses and Woodpigeons have frequently nested in the Wisteria. We recently put up some bird boxes to see if we could encourage more birds to nest there. We had some Blue Tits in one of the boxes this year (2022). A second box was also utilised. A Blackbird nested in the Wisteria so we had to delay pruning it for a while. All visiting birds would find an abundance of insects and seeds within the garden walls at different times of the year. The Robin, often in attendance whenever the gardening team carry out their maintenance work, ventured really close so as not to miss out on any tiny morsels that we have disturbed.

We were informed that a Sparrowhawk had dived down to grab a small bird which it plucked and ate below the Myrtle bush, though this didn't happen whilst the garden team were working. Following that occasion there were many small feathers strewn about and more under the Myrtle bush.

Image 23 The Friendly Robin. Photo taken late September 2015

FLOWERS

The 'Met Office' consider 1st March as the first day of spring. On 1st March 2010, amazingly, after a chilly start, it became a gloriously sunny day with barely a cloud in sight and it was a warm 10 degrees. By 11.00 a.m. the Crocus 'carpet' in this garden all opened up in the sunshine, together with many Snowdrops and some Snowflakes (*Leucojum*) and so the garden took on a magical sparkle. Interestingly in 2016 this show of flowers was to be seen as early as January, very possibly as a result of our changing climate.

The earliest spring flowers are quickly followed by Daffodils, Hellebores, Anemone, and the decorative Japanese Quince shrubs on the walls which flower prolifically are much loved by various bumblebees, particularly the biggest ones. Rosemary blooms and various herbs such as Greater Celandine, old Byzantium Gladioli, Irises and many more flowers in progression throughout every month that are attractive to a whole range of insects.

Some of the herbs in the garden are really wild flowers, like those used in the past for medicines such as Marsh Mallow, Tansy, Paeony (*P.officinalis*), and house-strewing herbs, such as Meadow Rue and Sweet Woodruff. There are also Evening Primrose, Mullein, Chicory, Violets, Lavender, Wall Germander, Cotton Lavender, Pasque Flower, Lungwort, Wormwood, Myrtle, Bay, Rosemary, Feverfew, Lemon Balm and so on. As you can imagine, all the plants listed have attracted a multitude of insects, particularly throughout the summer, and I have only been there to note a fraction of them. The older heavily scented flowers fill the air with lovely aromas, accompanied by the buzzing of bees and it is a joy to the senses.

INSECTS

I have watched and noted various insects over the seasons and years and I usually take photos of the more interesting ones whenever possible. All types of bees are in abundance as nearly all the plants are good for them to visit throughout the year from the earliest flowers on the flowering Quinces and Lungworts to the Salvias that continue flowering into the winter. The Buff-tailed Bumblebee Queen hibernates over winter in an old mouse nest or somewhere similar and emerges in spring to search for a source of much needed nectar. She does this before finding a new nesting site to continue her cycle of raising new bumblebees. The garden is visited by a huge variety of insects from really early in the year until the end of November. We have introduced a small bug hotel and have also assembled some larger log-lengths into a small wood-pile as winter accommodation for numerous insects and other small creatures.

Sometimes there has been an interesting surprise with the species of caterpillars or moths we have disturbed whilst gardening. One small attractive moth, commonly named the Mint Moth, has been living through its life-cycle in the garden for several years. Its colouring is mainly crimson with some gold markings. It has a small relative that has off-white markings on the hindwing that has also been seen. Finding these small moths has sparked off a general interest in moths, which hitherto, I had not really considered learning about: though I am always happy to gain knowledge of something new in the world of natural history. It would be good to lookout for the Mint Moth's dull green with black spotted larvae in the future probably feeding on Catmint and other Mints. These little moths fly both during the day or night with two broods per year. The adults may be seen flying in May-June and July-August. This moth has been seen in the garden for several years since first noticing it, and so I've concluded its whole life cycle has been sustained well in the Museum Garden. The food plants for the larvae are various Mints, Clary, Lemon Balm and Catmint which we do have in this garden.

Other moths found in the garden include the caterpillar, and later the adult, of the Elephant Hawk-moth, the Hummingbird Hawk-moth and the beautiful Grey Dagger Moth caterpillar, the latter being found on a shrub rose by one of the gardening team, and a Knot Grass caterpillar on an evergreen shrub.

As mentioned above, another spectacular caterpillar discovered on one of the roses last year was the Grey Dagger with a row of white along the base of the body and two red blotches on a black background along each segment and a yellow strip along the top with tufts of stiff hairs. The adult moth is unusually dull-looking with grey and brownish markings on the forewings and white hind wings. The range of food plants is wide but it also likes many deciduous trees and shrubs. There is only one generation per year and the caterpillars feed from August to early October. It pupates in the soil or rotten wood and the adult moth emerges in the following June. This may extend to two generations per year with climate warming, some being seen now in May.

Image 24 The Grey Dagger Moth caterpillar. Photo taken at the end of July 2017

Image 25 The Small Mint Moth on Tansy leaves. Photo taken September 2005

Several years ago, the Mullein leaves were destroyed, just leaving the main stem and flowers. An ugly sight. This damage was done by the Mullein Moth caterpillars. There was concern at the time that a foreign caterpillar looking very similar had been imported from abroad and found on Mullein. I checked that it was the genuine native Mullein Moth caterpillar in the Museum Garden. The eggs are laid on the food plant in April and May so the caterpillars are active up to July. They pupate in cocoons in the soil.

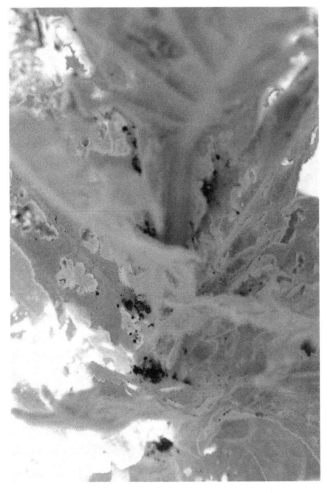

Image 26 The Mullein Moth caterpillars completely destroyed the appearance of the Mullein plant and its flowers. This was in June 2011

On a lovely sunny September morning we watched an adult Hummingbird Hawk-moth, on a red-flowered Salvia shrub: such a thrill to watch as it hovered to gather nectar. The caterpillars feed mostly on Bedstraws.

Images 27 & 28 Hummingbird Hawk-moth adult in September 2016. Below: A Knot Grass caterpillar

Some years ago, we also found a huge Elephant Hawk-moth caterpillar around the Bedstraw area. Later, during that autumn, I accidently disturbed an adult Elephant Hawk-moth, clothed in its splendid pale olive green and pink patterns, in some Woodruff. I was surprised to see it flying during the day. The large caterpillar of that species when young are green but as they mature they become a blackish brown and usually feed at night. Their choice food plants include Willowherbs, Evening Primrose, and Fuchsias when in gardens, all of which we have in the Museum Garden. The pupae overwinter in the soil and the adult, beautiful green and pink moths emerge in summer flying mostly at night.

On some evergreen leaves, we found a Knot Grass caterpillar. It was covered in long brown hairs and it was quite a short caterpillar. We left it to munch away in peace because of its long hairs which could easy bring on an allergic rash. Generally, this caterpillar can be found from May and again in August as mentioned in Chapter One, and it relies on Dock, Plantain and Hop as its food plants. There is a Golden Hop plant in the Museum Garden.

In late summer, a White Ermine Moth caterpillar was noticed on some Phlox leaves. The caterpillar feeds on a wide range of low growing herbaceous plants. The pupa exists in a grey silky cocoon among leaf litter on the ground until the following May. The adult moths are a ghostly white with dainty black spots and a yellow abdomen but the larva is dark brown and hairy with a red line along its back.

When gardening it is so lovely to see butterflies flitting around the garden on sunny days. Seen throughout their relevant seasons are the Brimstone, Peacock, Orange-tip, Small Tortoiseshell, Red Admiral, the Common Blue, Holly Blue, and the Small Copper. In the spring it is lovely to see the first Brimstone, which often appears in March showing you that spring is really underway. The male is more noticeable as it is a darker hue than the pale female. They are single-brooded butterflies seen in April and May, but any seen flying in August and September are the offspring that will hibernate until increased daylight and the warmth of the sun tempts them to emerge in March the following year.

Usually, the next butterfly to spot would be the Orange-tip, in April and June. The male has the orange tips to the forewings and the female has black wing tips and she lays an orange egg on the flower stem of either the Cuckoo-flower or Garlic Mustard. The green and white larvae eat the seedpods of most of the Cabbage family plants which we have here in the garden.

In May the Small Copper, can be seen basking on flowers in the garden. It has orange forewings with some black spots and a pale brown wing margin though this butterfly may be seen for several months, since it is double-brooded.

The Common Blue Butterfly, may be seen from April to September as it has more than one brood. The male is blue whilst the female is brown with orange markings near the edge of the wings.

The Peacock Butterfly awakes from hibernation in the warmth of spring and may be seen throughout the summer months. It is easily recognisable with its large 'false eyes' on each of the colourful wings.

The Small Tortoiseshell and the Red Admiral also awake from hibernation in spring sunshine. The later broods seen can be the ones that hibernated over winter, though additional ones also travel here from abroad. The Red Admiral is actually seen during most months of the year. There has been a slight increase in the number of Small Tortoiseshell Butterflies in the 2022 season.

The Holly Blue may be seen flying in April and May and in August and September. The larvae feed on Holly in spring and Ivy in winter, and we have plenty of Ivy plants available here on various walls.

Whilst working in the Museum Garden on summer days, apart from butterflies, we have the added bonus of noticing ladybirds, caterpillars, moths, bees and other insects as we are working there. We also have a great succession of flowering herbs and other plants for them to enjoy nectar throughout all the seasons.

A large number of different Ladybirds have been present: some of them the non-native Harlequin ones. During the winter they hide within old flower stalks and shrivelled leaves till the warmth in the spring warmth wakes them up. So, it is a good practice not to cut down all old spent growth in autumn. Ladybirds are good for the garden as they eat aphids, and scale insects. Unfortunately, the Harlequin Ladybirds are likely to eat our native species' larvae as well as moth and butterfly eggs, too.

The Common Green Lacewing is often spotted in all our gardens. Lacewings are a gardener's friend too, as the larvae feed on aphids,

Image 29 The more familiar butterflies: top left clockwise: Small Tortoiseshell, Peacock, Holly Blue, Common Blue, Brimstone and Orange-tip

caterpillars and insect eggs on the foliage. The adult Lacewings only visit plants for nectar and pollen. They have antennae, and two pairs of transparent wings which are held over their body when they are resting. They live among the taller herbaceous plants, grasses or hedges.

Among the 'pest' category of insects I should mention the Rose Sawfly larvae which devour rose leaves and, in a bad year, has denuded whole areas of the Rose 'Buff Beauty' foliage on the rear wall. This Sawfly's larvae conceal themselves in curled leaves and munch away defoliating quite a few areas of the rose leaves. The adult sawflies have a yellow abdomen and black thorax. These Sawflies have not as yet attacked other roses around the garden.

The plant itself is unaffected except for its untidy, bare appearance. Another pest frequently seen, is the larvae of the Solomon Seal Sawfly, which can quickly defoliate this whole plant. The small larva is grey with a black head.

A pest that can't be missed is the bright scarlet-red Lily Beetle. Whilst they don't kill the Lilies, they make such a slimy, dirty mess on them so that the plants look almost destroyed. We have always picked off any adult Lily Beetles by hand (and crushed them) whenever we've discovered them, which has usually been on a sunny morning between April and July. The larvae also need to be watched out for in May to September, as the ugly orange and black larvae hatch from eggs laid on the underside of the leaves which they then eat. These pests can also occur on Fritillary plants.

I should also mention that we encountered the destructive Box Tree Moth caterpillars during 2019. They were first found in British gardens in 2011 after establishing in London and spreading to the South-East Region. Now they have been found in other regions of the British Isles. The caterpillars become active when the weather warms up from March onwards and operate under a mass of webbing, defoliating Box bushes. After pupation the adults lay eggs in May to start the process again. The adult moth is usually noticed as it is mostly white with a brown border to the wings, though it can be in other forms of all white or all brown. The caterpillars are yellow with black markings on top and a two black stripes along the whole body. It would seem the Box bushes in the Museum Garden survived their first attack and were fully leaved the following year. Though, due to the Coronavirus pandemic and long periods of lockdown throughout 2020 and during January to the end of March 2021, the team have not been to the garden very often. Should signs of this Box bush pest be seen again it can now be controlled but with chemicals, but we do not use any in this garden. Another defoliation could weaken the bushes so much that they would need to be destroyed. There are natural predators of these caterpillars which include parasitic wasps and flies, ants and spiders and maybe some birds as well. However, in summer 2021 we noticed that the Box Tree caterpillars were back once more and since then I have spotted an adult Box Tree Moth in November. Unfortunately, in the summer of 2022 we had to dig up and remove both Box plants and will replace them with something different.

In August 2017 some visitors to the garden were agitated as they spotted what they insisted was a Hornet. However, I took a photo of it and have since been assured it was a Hornet 'mimic' (of which there are many types which hope to scare off their own predators with warning colours as Wasps or Hornets). By name, this one was *Volucella zonaria*, which is in fact a Hoverfly. Its larvae scavenge a living in Wasp nests.

Common Wasps which are generally not loved by people, should be welcomed by gardeners in the early and mid-summer as they

Image 30 The Hornet-like Hoverfly. Photo taken in July 2017

Images 31 & 32 A wasp-mimic Hoverfly on a Cupid's Dart flower in 2015. Below: Another Hoverfly wasp-mimic

feed on aphids and other insects, but it is in late Summer that the adults turn to sweet things and nectar and that is when we find them annoying us by eating jam, sweet apples and so on. One year we had a Wasps' nest in one of the compost heaps at the back of the Museum so we needed caution when adding garden waste to the adjoining bins.

There are many insects that mimic Wasps or Bees, and one is the Marmalade Hoverfly, which has a rather attractive orange and black band pattern on the abdomen. The adults are nectar feeders and the larvae eat aphids – so quite useful to a gardener. I have seen it in the Museum Garden on several occasions. There are many similar insects, though some don't have common names, but only have long botanical names: most of them have yellow and black patterns on their abdomens.

Plant Galls are abnormal growths or swellings found on plants and some are caused by tiny insects. There are many different types of Galls, some of them not frequently noticed. Among the most common though, is the so-called Robin's Pincushion, also

Image 33 Robin's Pincushion Galls in the Museum Garden, late August 2014

known as the Rose Bedeguar Gall. This particular Gall is caused by a small Gall Wasp, causing an abnormal growth on a rose and looking like a ball of moss. The adult lays eggs in chambers inside the ball structure and the grubs grow, over-winter, and emerge as adults the following May. This Gall is to be found on roses and has been seen in the Museum Garden though I don't believe it does harm to the plants, but looks quite odd.

FAUNA

Apart from a squirrel or two, and maybe a fox, there are not really many animals likely to visit the walled garden. Hedgehogs wouldn't be able to find a way in and in nineteen years I have never found evidence of any. There are probably Wood Mice about somewhere towards the back of the Museum near the compost bins.

I have yet to hunt for spiders in this garden, so I have no idea as yet what species of spider might be on site with the exception of an autumn Common Garden Spider. However, new book in hand, I am going to investigate how many species I can find as time goes on.

Of the non-wild animals there are two cats that regularly visit, though I personally do not welcome them as I suspect they intend to catch a songbird or two.

FUNGI

We do often get Mildew occurring especially in a hot dry summer because we have some really old varieties of roses that are prone to Mildew. One such is the 'Souvenir de la Malmaison' which is a pretty pale pink Bourbon Rose created by Jean Béluze in 1843. Most modern-day species are often engineered to be mildew-free varieties. Mildew occurs when the plants do not have sufficient water under hot dry conditions and when there is not much

Images 34 & 35 Above: The Museum Garden in full growth: July 2017
Below: The Millais Bronze: *Fighting Game Birds* in the Museum Garden
John G Millais, son of J Everett Millais, was a local artist and Naturalist

airflow round the plant. The garden team are not always able to water often enough in the garden, though we do try to call in and water as often as we can. Black Spot is another unwelcome fungus, and some of the roses have exhibited the unsightly black spots. We try to garden organically, so we have not sprayed plants to avoid this fungus. Fortunately, we haven't experienced any Honey Fungus but have seen one or two other types of fungus in the garden.

CHAPTER THREE
HORSHAM'S GREEN SPACES

Any of the larger local Green Spaces are good for investigating what nature visits or inhabits them. In 2013 a survey had shown there to be 101 named Green Spaces around the town and its outskirts. Though very more recently some of them have been considered for new housing by the Council. As a personal view, I am not sure how this does not conflict with the Council also currently working with the Sussex Wildlife Trust on eco systems and preserving natural history in the area. Usually, any Green Spaces being considered for housing stirs local people to actively protest and present really good reasons why such buildings would be inappropriate and most likely to destroy our precious wildlife systems and corridors. It also decreases the opportunities for local people to enjoy Green Spaces for their leisure time, whilst the population of Horsham has increased quite rapidly with the increased housing already completed. It is well known now that the great outdoors is extremely good for our mental wellbeing and this has never been so important as in the last two years with the Covid global pandemic adversely affecting all of us.

THE POND ON COOTES GREEN

My nearest Green Space used to be the Cootes Pond. This small area around a few shops and a crescent of housing was registered as a Village Green early in the 2000s. Historically, this area used to be the site of Cootes Farm house before all the Davis estates were built in the 1950s. Being a small pond, it cannot sustain more than a few breeding wildfowl, though it does it become a temporary daytime home to many Ducks, Geese, Moorhens, Coots and Gulls, most of whom roost at the Warnham Local Nature Reserve around sunset.

Image 36 Cootes Pond: An acrylic painting of wildlife there by the author

In February 2016, I counted 48 Mallards and 13 Canada Geese plus many Gulls and a Moorhen plus a few other species of duck at the pond side. It was a frosty but sunny morning. I took a photo of some of the ducks and later, when I examined it, I was surprised to see that amongst the female Mallards, there was a male Shoveler Duck in 'Eclipse' plumage, that is, not yet in male breeding plumage. A few years later I noticed there was often a Chinese Mandarin Duck visiting with the Mallards. The first time I saw it I concluded it was a youngster, but it returned again the following year, though I never saw it with a partner.

Whilst the Shoveler is a common winter visitor it is unlikely to breed here in the UK but migrates to Northern Europe and as far as the Baltic regions. Its large bill is used to filter plankton from shallow, muddy pools.

Image 37 Shoveler Drake in Eclipse Plumage – Cootes Pond, taken February 2016

The Mandarin Duck was seen several times usually with some Mallard Ducks around the pond. Originally from China, the Mandarins were introduced to English wildfowl collectors in the 1700's but many escaped or were released in the 1900s and they have been found in Sussex since 1965. Several pairs can usually be seen at the Warnham Local Nature Reserve. Typically, of wood-ducks they nest in tree cavities. In winter they like to eat beechmast, acorns and sweet chestnuts.

FUNGI

I have only taken note of one of the most recognised and colourful red Fly Agaric Fungus, in the grass near a Silver Birch tree on the Green, though I suspect there are plenty of other common fungi present as well were I to look more diligently. The Fly Agaric can

Image 38 Lonely Mandarin Duck – Cootes Green Pond area, taken early May 2018

Image 39 Canada Geese with young Goslings, Cootes Pond, taken late July 2004

be seen from late summer into autumn and may turn yellowish as they age and the white scales may disappear, especially after heavy rain. When they are fresh, they cannot really be mistaken for any other type of fungus. It contains an acid which is a weak insecticide and used to be used since medieval times as a fly-killer. Please note that Fly Agaric is poisonous, and you should always wash your hands if you handle any fungi.

Fairly recently, I think, that one of the trees around the pond had displayed the very undesirable Honey Fungus, which meant that the tree had to be removed and replaced with a more resistant species of tree. Honey Fungus, kills many trees and spreads out underground in a radius from the infected tree and therefore may do more damage to other trees. It is very difficult to put any kind of barrier down to prevent the spread happening under the ground. Earth can be dug out and disposed of. Honey Fungus grows in clusters on or around the base of the tree and is

Image 40 Fly Agaric Fungi – Cootes Green, taken late October 2014

widespread throughout the country. It can be seen between July and December.

ANOTHER GREEN SPACE: THE ROOKWOOD AREA.
(This area was under review recently by HDC: see Appendix1, and is now termed an important space for local people and wildlife, 2021.)

This is a fairly large area of land much used by local people in their leisure time to wander through for dog walking, cycling and there is an eighteen-hole golf course too. There are two rivers; the man-made Red River, and the Boldings Brook which flow through this area. The Red River was made to carry away water from the sluices of the Warnham Nature Reserve millpond. There is also a man-made lake on part of the golf course. There are trees, shrubs, hedges and many wild flowers throughout the seasons,

Image 41 A Frosty Autumn View at Rookwood in 2004

all creating a great natural corridor for birds, insects and plants on the way up to the local Nature Reserve across the Warnham Road.

BIRDS

I walked this whole area twice a day for five years as a dog walker, though after that era, I have often walked through Rookwood up to the local Nature Reserve. Along the Red River path, I have seen Blackbirds, Thrushes, Robins, Long-tailed Tits, Great Tits, a Greater Spotted Woodpecker, Woodpigeons, Magpies and Rooks. One time, I saw a very vocal group of about a dozen Nuthatches all together in a section of hedge and large shrubs along the riverside. I have seen Kingfishers that have nested in a sandy bank by one of the bridges, and have also heard Treecreepers nearby though they are difficult to spot in their camouflage brown feathers. Sometimes though, you suddenly catch sight of movement, or their pale breast, as happened to me recently.

Treecreepers are small birds with a brown, speckled back and a pale front, and can be difficult to spot since they are well camouflaged on tree bark. Their habit is to fly down near the base of a trunk and then progress up the tree in a circular manner round and round all the time probing for insects and spiders with their fine, downward curved bill. Their tail is used as a prop for stability on the trunk and their claws are large and curved too. Once at the top of a tree, they fly down to another trunk to repeat the process. If you listen hard, you might hear their song which is a high-pitched string of notes. I think it is somewhat similar to a Goldcrest song which is also high-pitched, but in phrased sequence. Treecreepers nest in cavities underneath loose bark.

Kingfishers are so brightly coloured in their flashy blue and orange feathers but you still may not notice them if they are in dappled shade near a pond or river. They may attract your attention by the sharp ringing call they make often when flying low above the surface of a river or pond. If you are lucky enough to see one, the flash of blue as they dart along is so amazing. If you know their usual perches and route you may be able to observe them for much longer. I've watched one for more than twenty minutes on a couple of occasions. They dive for small fish or aquatic insects. Even better, if you know where they are nesting, but never disturb any nesting bird. They dig out a small round tunnel in an earth or sandy-soiled bank in which to lay eggs and brood their young.

On a late May evening nature walk with a few members of a local Natural History Society we walked to the accompaniment of many birds singing away as we weaved along the Boldings Brook river path: there were Chiffchaffs, Blackcaps, a Robin, Blue Tits, Long-tailed Tits, Blackbirds, a Wren and Garden Warbler.

Additionally, there was also a Mistle Thrush singing away in the evening twilight in a group of tall trees. Its song is loud and clear, sung in short phrases, but a less repetitive song than the Song Thrush's repertoire. Mistle Thrushes are larger birds and the breast spots, dark and more rounded than those of Song Thrushes.

FLOWERS

Walking along the Red River path amongst some trees and shrubs there were Bluebells (mixed: some English and some Spanish), Greater Stitchwort, and a few Ramsons (Wild Garlic). The place to see a multitude of Ramsons is in a different direction along the main Horsham Riverside Walk leaving the Rookwood walk over the Millennium Bridge and turn right to follow the river which is behind the Cootes Avenue houses. Within a few hundred yards, there is an area locally named 'Onion Island' where in late May, the area is a mass of Ramsons and you can smell garlic before you get there. The Bluebells are also hybridising and thus endangering our native more delicate English Bluebell, which has thinner leaves and the flowers hang daintily in an arc. The Spanish Bluebell, has much thicker, wider leaves and the flowers are around an upright stem.

We walked around the perimeter of the golf course lake but disappointingly, on that occasion, there were no wildfowl on the lake at all as they had probably roosted somewhere by that time, but we added some flowers to our list. These were, Black Medick, Gorse, Red Clover, Bitter Vetchling and Birds-foot Trefoil. Black Medick, which I hadn't known of before, looks an untidy plant with clusters of leaflets along an upright stem and has yellow spherical flowers from April onwards. After fruiting it has distinctive black coiled seed pods. Bitter Vetchling has upright growth with narrow leaflets which end in a point and not tendrils like some in the pea family. The Flowers are a dusky red and they fade to blue. Birds-foot Trefoil, is a low growing plant with yellow to orange flowers. It is also commonly named 'Eggs and Bacon' and blooms from May onwards. The Common Blue Butterfly larvae feed on this and related plants.

There was also so plenty of white Blackthorn blossom along the hedge-line shrubs. This blossom occurs before the leaves appear

Image 42 Path through the Onion Island Area: Ramsons Galore! photo taken in April 2011

and, later in the autumn, the purple berries are known as sloes. The Hawthorn leaves were only just emerging as they flower later on, after the leaves appear. The Hawthorn flower is known to have a foul smell and later has red berries, known as haws. Sometimes people confuse these two shrubs since both produce white flowers though at slightly different times, as I have described. One year I saw the Common Holly in flower in the same area and I admit I had never noticed the white holly flowers before. These trees have either male or female flowers, so all Hollies with berries are female trees. We all know the red berries when we see them prior to the Christmas period, but I was pleased to have seen the white flowers in the spring.

Using the alley entrance in Merryfield Drive, and walking from the Millennium Bridge in May time, you can find: Cowslips, Goose Grass – also known as Cleavers, Tufted Vetch, Garlic Mustard – also known as Jack-by-the-Hedge, Guelder Rose, Red Campion, Bugle, Chicory, Ground Ivy and Cow Parsley.

This path takes you to the Redford Road exit, but if you carry on along the Boldings Brook banks there are large clumps of Rosebay Willowherb, which flowers from June to September, and this brings you to a large sloping field area named locally as Leggyfield, which also borders on the Warnham Road area. Following this path, it bends and rises till you walk alongside a hedged area by the Red River. On the way you can find large patches of Speedwell, Stitchwort, Buttercups, Nettles and some Holly shrubs. By the hedge-line is a bush of Broom on the way to the Warnham Road exit.

Cowslips may be seen from April into May noticeable by their yellow cup-like flowers cluster at the top of a tall stem with a rosette of wrinkle-edged, primrose-like leaves that sharply taper to the base of the stem. Cowslips have orange markings toward the base of the lobes and the flower cluster usually droops to one side on downy stalks. False Oxlips are a hybrid between the Primrose and the Cowslip: it has more primrose-yellow flower clusters,

Image 43 Merryfield Drive path to Millennium Bridge, Rookwood on a winter dog-walk

shorter stalks and the leaves taper more gradually to the base. It can be easy to confuse these plants. Garlic Mustard, is a common biennial hedgerow plant, preferring a sheltered place to thrive. It has white four-petalled flowers in April to June and heart-shaped, toothed leaves. If crushed, it smells slightly of garlic. The Orange-tip Butterfly often lays an egg on Garlic Mustard as an alternative to the Cuckoo-flower.

The Guelder Rose actually belongs to Honeysuckle family, and its appearance is very similar to the Red Currant bushes grown in gardens but do not be fooled. The Guelder Rose has white umbel flowers with some larger white sterile flowers on the edge and small flowers at the centre of the umbel and later on, red, translucent berries. The leaves turn red before they drop. A Red Currant bush has yellow/green, red-edged flowers held in clusters, but later on, similar looking red berries.

Image 44 Marsh Marigolds by the Millennium Bridge, Rookwood. Photo taken in 2012

A large clump of Marsh Marigold, was flowering profusely with bright yellow buttercup-like flowers at the edge of the brook by the Millennium Bridge when exiting the walk back into Merryfield Drive. However, in a 2021 visit, I was sorry to see only a small Marsh Marigold clump in the same spot.

Image 45 Stitchwort in Leggyfield, August 2004

Later in the year in the Leggyfield area there were many Buttercups, Plantains and Thyme-leaved Speedwell. Also, the Gorse and Broom on the top path and as we turned to go back by Boldings Brook there were large patches of Speedwell and Stitchwort. On our left was a huge patch of tall stinging nettles just about flowering but with no apparent sign of caterpillars. Several butterflies use stinging nettles as their food plant: the Peacock, Small Tortoiseshell,

Image 46 Wood Anemones at Rookwood, April 2017

Red Admiral and the Comma. Some moths do so as well. Further along we found Wild Celery, Tufted Vetch and a Small Blue and a White Butterfly. Also, some Wild Carrot, Cow Parsley, Garlic Mustard, and Foxgloves.

Other plants also found in the main Rookwood area include Wood Anemones that form a white carpet in woodland from March to May. The white flowers sometimes tinged with pale colour, and the leaves are trifoliate. Burdock is a biennial and has huge almost heart-shaped leaves which in its second spring, sends up very tall stems with purple flowers with bracts that are hooked they cling on to people's clothing, or animals' fur. Dog's Mercury, is an unattractive plant that many people are inclined to overlook. These plants are either male or female. The male has catkins and the female flowers are tiny, purple with white bracts. It is a poisonous plant which grows on shady banks and grows in woodland in great numbers and it is also not good for livestock to eat.

INSECTS

In May you can often see very tiny green caterpillars dangling from Oak trees some of them are the larvae of the Winter Moth. There are also other small caterpillars that dangle from Oak trees, such as the Green Oak Tortrix Moth. I have not investigated very much about Oak trees and the huge number of species that live on it, but I read a book entitled 'Oakwatch' many years ago which was devoted to just that subject: all the natural history in and around the Oak tree.

A Gall was found on a small Oak along on the path leading back to the Millennium Bridge. It was a mature Oak Marble Gall which was brown and woody. They are green when immature. The asexual female Gall Wasp would have laid an egg in the Oak bud in the spring on the common Oak. The process differs when laid in Turkey Oak buds where the small Galls form but the larvae are bisexual. There maybe 70 different Gall Wasp species on Oaks – with a cycle far too complicated for me to understand. More well-known are the Spangle Galls which are found on the underside of the Oak leaf, but this Gall is produced by a different species of Gall Wasp – again rather too complicated to explain here, plus I need to learn more about their life cycles myself.

There are food plants enjoyed by several species of butterfly. The Garlic Mustard is a food plant for the caterpillars of the Green-veined White, as well as the Orange-tip. The Green-veined White Butterfly has two broods in April to May and July to August, and lays its yellow eggs on to the Garlic Mustard or other Cabbage family plants.

FAUNA

I have to mention that I thought I had seen a Water Vole near the Millennium Bridge twelve years ago, but that would be most unlikely so must conclude I was mistaken and was probably an ordinary Rat. However, I did see a Mink, (definitely non-native)

Image 47 Garlic Mustard, Rookwood, with 7-spot Ladybird. Photo taken April 2012

between there and the next exit bridge to Redford Road which I did report because Mink are not welcome animals because they cause havoc with our true native water-based birds and animals, especially in the nearby Nature Reserve.

It used to be quite easy to see frogspawn in various streams and ditches around Rookwood particularly in slow running areas of the Boldings Brook. Sometimes local children would collect jam jars of them and take them home to see their progression through all the tadpole stages. Other wildlife also predate the tadpoles which is why the frogs have to lay so much spawn in order to secure the next generation.

Walking through 'Onion Island' and onwards towards the Guildford Road which is part of the local 'Riverside Walk', I once found a dead Mole in the middle of the wooded path. I concluded that maybe a dog had toyed with it although it appeared to be in perfect condition.

Image 48 A peaceful sunset at the Rookwood Lake, one August evening

Deer can be seen all around this area and they are occasionally noticed on the golf course.

* *

Please see Appendix 1 for details of the recent HDC intention to put up to 1000 houses on the Rookwood Site and how local organisations and the public put strong views against using this area for housing. The loss of this area would have been tragic for all the wildlife that uses Rookwood as a corridor to the Nature Reserve as well as a great loss of a well-used and enjoyed public space and golf course. In 2021 HDC agreed to withdraw plans for housing here and acknowledged that this is an important Green Space for Horsham residents. Author.

* *

CHAPTER FOUR

WARNHAM LOCAL NATURE RESERVE

The land of this Reserve was dedicated for a local Nature Reserve in 1988. It is a real bonus for Horsham people to have this Reserve less than ten minutes away from Horsham town, and for me it is only a short walk away. The Reserve covers approximately 92 acres and includes many different habitats: woodland, meadow, damp (boggy) reed beds, the main millpond and several small ponds, scrapes and Boldings Brook. In the half-term holiday in October 2021 a new Discovery Hub was opened affording great views out over the millpond area.

Hence the range of wildlife found there encompasses woodland birds and waterfowl, including some unusual avian visitors from time to time. Mammals from Deer to Dormice, Wild Flowers (about 400 plant species). Insects of all sorts: Dragonflies and Damselflies, Butterflies and Moths, Flies, Beetles and Bugs. As part of the current Management Plan some sheep (dark coloured Hebridean and the white and woolly Herdwick) and British White Cattle are used at appropriate times of the year to graze some of the different habitats: sheep in the flower meadow, and cattle in the wet meadow.

I have wandered around the Reserve on numerous occasions over the last eighteen years and so for the purpose of this chapter I have tried to compile my sightings from masses of notes taken at different seasons of the year.

BIRDS

Each time you go to the Reserve you cannot anticipate what birds you will see. Sometimes, unexpectedly something unusual flies in

Image 49 WLNR Millpond August 2018

Image 50 A view of the New Discovery Hub February 2021 when still under construction

Image 51 Sheep in the Flower Meadow in February 2021

and words spreads rapidly nowadays on social media, so then the Reserve is crowded with extra birdwatchers, complete with their long-lens cameras, binoculars and telescopes. I have been fortunate over the years to have been able to catch a fleeting look at a Honey Buzzard, a Goosander, a Mediterranean Gull, and more recently, a Little Bunting. In 2021 there was a visit from an Osprey and I can recall a similar fleeting visit of one a few years previously. There are other less common birds that have now come to the millpond area like Water Rail, Snipe, a pair of Egyptian Geese, the Little Egrets and recently, the Large Egret. In recent times some Mandarin Ducks have bred on the millpond, as have a pair of Terns. A Water Rail is well camouflaged in reeds at the edge of the millpond, but I have only once caught sight of it.

A good selection of birds can be seen regularly in the millpond. Some are year-round residents and some visit in summer or winter:

Coots, Moorhens, Mallards, Mandarin Ducks, Cormorants, a Shoveler, Teals, Wigeons, a pair of Swans (sometimes a third Swan), Greylag Geese, a pair of Egyptian Geese, Black-headed, Black-backed, Herring and Common Gulls, a pair of Common Terns, Great Crested Grebes, Small Grebes (Dabchicks), Tufted Ducks, Pochards and a Water Rail.

On a slightly damp and misty January morning songbirds were singing in the trees: in particular the Robin, Blue Tit, Great Tit and the Wren. It was soggy and slippery underfoot, as floods from before Christmas had subsided leaving a trail of silt, especially visible on the board-walk area, so not surprisingly there were several Mallard Ducks puddling about.

In 2014 a male Goosander in breeding plumage, visited the millpond before moving on to its breeding ground. I enjoyed the challenge of painting this unusual duck and my painting is included with a few others at the end of this book. The Goosander is a diving duck and it has a sawbill which enables it to catch and hold on to its fish-prey more easily. The female is grey with a white wing-patch and throat with a white chin patch. These ducks prefer freshwater and usually nest in waterside trees.

Having watched a Shoveler Duck at the Reserve one January I was really pleased to see it later on in full plumage during March. It has a large, heavy bill and the male has yellow eyes and a large rust-colour on the body with white flanks and orange legs. The female looks similar to a female Mallard, but still has the large bill.

Grey Herons are seen often, because of their large size and they are also impressive in flight. In the past there used to be herons nesting high in the trees nearest the millpond, though more recently they have nested further back out of sight. Usually though, they can be seen standing very still at the edge of the millpond and then suddenly stabbing small fish or frog to eat. One year, 2016 I think, there were about a dozen herons all in one tree that I thought looked a little like a 'Heron Clock'! It was wonderful to see so many of them together in one place. I'm not sure lately whether there have been fewer resident herons due to changing conditions in the millpond; for example, it being shallower nowadays; or maybe there are fewer fish.

Image 52 About a dozen Herons in the tree at the back of the Millpond

Another sizeable bird is the Cormorant, which frequently perch near the top of a tree opposite the 'Heron Hide', or after having dip and dive in millpond they sometimes perch on the rafts with their wings outstretched to preen and dry off. These birds can be seen all year round at the Reserve, diving in the millpond and catching fish. They have a white patch near their hook-tipped bill and iridescent black feathers on their backs. Juveniles have white fronts which confused me in identifying them correctly at first. Usually, the Whooper Swans have nested on a flat platform

Images 53 & 54 Swan and Cygnets in June and (below) in December 2016

amongst the reeds and many times they have successfully raised a young family. It is lovely to see the cygnets grow up and mature, The Pochard, a gregarious freshwater duck, can often be seen in company with Tufted Ducks. The male Pochard has a dark front and back, pale sides, with a rusty-coloured head and red-eyes.

The Tufted Ducks are smaller diving ducks and the bill is bluish with a black tip. They mostly eat water plants and insects. The male has a black body with white patches on the sides and yellow eyes. He has a tuft or crest on the back of his head. The female is brown with buff sides. They often are in mixed flocks with other ducks.

The Dabchick or Little Grebe, is an attractive small water-bird with a small white spot at the base of the thick bill and has rufous cheeks in breeding season. It has no visible tail and is a poor flyer. It eats small fish, molluscs, insects and their larvae – all caught underwater. It may carry its young on its back.

In 2014, I spent some time appreciating a Grey Wagtail, that has raised a family on the Reserve as they have now for several years since. It was often seen from the first Hide near the sluice gates of the millpond though I also saw it from the boardwalk in the Boldings Brook area, near the wet meadow.

On a couple of occasions, I have seen a Kingfisher on a derelict tree overhanging the Boldings Brook where I have stood quietly and watched it for several minutes, though most sightings have been from the 'Heron Hide' and the fairly new 'Aston Trelford Hide'. When Kingfishers have young to feed and both parents are busy collecting food for them, I feel very fortunate to have watched them for about twenty minutes. I will never tire of watching these beautiful birds. Sometimes after a lot of rain, the water has been too murky for the Kingfisher to dive for fish in the millpond.

From the boardwalk facing the wet meadow, there are several old Willows and once I sat quietly watching a Treecreeper slip behind some loose bark on one of them to feed its young in the nest there.

Image 55 Grey Wagtail. Photo taken in 2014

Only a few months ago, I saw five Treecreepers on an ivy-clad tree at the rear of the millpond area. That was a great bonus for me.

Walking along the wooded section where some fir trees were, I have heard and seen Goldcrests, and Long-tailed Tits on numerous occasions, but I have also seen a Jay in that area. I frequently used to see Jays in the countryside during my childhood, but I rarely see them nowadays. They belong to the Corvid family but are attractive with their neat blue wing patches and dusky-pink plumage with a white rump. They feast on nuts, acorns, seeds and berries. Occasionally they eat tiny mammals or birds and eggs as well. In autumn they bury or hide acorns for later use. Like other Corvids their call is a harsh, screeching sound.

On some occasions there seemed little going on at the bird feeding station: just a few Chaffinches, Blue Tits and Great Tits, and sometimes a Nuthatch as well. There's plenty of birdsong to hear all around the Reserve and quite early in the year, sometimes in January and I have also heard the Greater Spotted Woodpecker drumming from a tall pole-like perch. Yet on another visit to the feeding station there were Siskins, Redpoll, Goldfinches, with Chaffinches, a Brambling and a Dunnock on the ground. In winter you may often see a male Pheasant in his smartest plumage and some females as well. The Great Spotted Woodpecker also comes in for some of the fat pressed into a tall stump. I once took a short video of a Blackbird that kept springing up and jumping to try to get some of the fat from the same tall stump. I was quite surprised to see it attempt that many times with occasional success. I have heard the 'yaffle' of the Green Woodpecker from the wooded area, though have seldom seen it.

One April visit two Red Kites flew over the millpond area causing small birds to be silent and hide in vegetation until the Kites had gone. This also happened when any birds of prey are about, though usually these were Buzzards. Nowadays you should be able to see to see the Great Crested Grebes, several Herons, Cormorants and sometimes a Little Egret on most visits. All the usual songbirds were about: Robins, Wrens, Great Tits, Blue Tits, Long-tailed Tits, and Chiffchaffs, Blackcaps and Nuthatches.

There are, of course, many other birds, large and small, that I have not mentioned or described. However, I must say a few words about the Great Crested Grebes, as they are so beautiful and each season raise some young which have stripes down the face and neck and sometimes, they hitch a ride on a parent's back. In spring the adults have chestnut ruffs and perform wonderful mating 'dances' and rituals – a marvel to watch.

FLOWERS

The flower meadow would be a great place to start looking for a good variety of plants.

Yellow Rattle is an annual, semi-parasitic plant of the Broomrape family, that lessens the presence of grasses over time and helps the meadow flowers establish with less competition from the grasses. It does not make chlorophyll but takes water and minerals from the grasses' roots. The leaves are opposite, without stalks, spear-shaped and toothed. It has yellow tubular flowers with an upper and lower lip with two short, violet teeth, which flower from May to July and produces seed pods later on. Seed capsules are produced later on and the seeds tend to rattle in the wind which is how the common name occurred.

Common Ragwort flowers between April and November. It is poisonous to many animals, but used by the caterpillars of the brightly striped Cinnabar Moth as its food plant. The yellow flowers are in branched, daisy-like clusters at the top of the plant, The leaves are deeply lobed, hairy underneath and clasping the stem.

Devil's-bit Scabious is another meadow summer flowering plant. It has a rhizome that sends up narrow long stalks for the domed, lilac-blue flowerheads that have stamens protruding out from the 'dome'. The leaves are in a basal rosette with other narrower leaves in opposite pairs further up the stem.

Wild Carrot has a long thin tap root, and the leaves are fern-like. The flowers are produced on flattish white-to-lilac umbels that have a sterile reddish flower at the centre. It has deeply divided leafy bracts below the flowers.

Meadow Cranesbill is an easily recognisable common field flower. The stems are red and hairy and the leaves are many-lobed, almost cut to the base. The flowers are blue-violet but the petals are not notched. The seed stalks bend down when ripe and the pods end with a long point hence the Cranes-bill's common name. Over a period of time, this plant forms noticeable clumps of blue coloured flowers in the meadow. Additionally, in the meadow area you may see Red Clover, Yarrow, Silverweed, Birds-foot Trefoil, Tufted

Vetch, Common Knapweed and, during May, June and July, the Common Spotted Orchid.

The Common Spotted Orchid has three pink or purple petals and three pink or purple sepals (varying in colour) that form a cone shape. The lowest petal is elongated. The red markings on the flowers are like dots and dashes. Spear-shaped leaves grow from a basal rosette and are blotched with purple spots. They do not always flower every year and the colour of the flowers may vary.

In the damper areas around the Reserve, you can find plants like Meadowsweet, which has tall stems with creamy-white frothy masses of blooms with a sweet and sickly scent. It flowers from June till September. Additionally, in wet areas there is Hemlock Water Dropwort, which has white domed umbels and the leaves

Image 56 Wild Carrot in the meadow area WLNR. Photo taken in August 2018

Image 57 Marsh Marigold clump in the reeds in March 2017

are compound, divided into segments, (similar looking to parsley leaves, but this plant is poisonous). It is also in flower from June to September. There is a large clump of Marsh Marigold among the reed beds, which should flower from March to July, though recently I found it beginning to flower as early as January. It has such lovely bright, shiny large buttercup-like flower and heart-shaped leaves and was also described in the Rookwood chapter.

Along the hedgerows and paths there are many plants to see, but some of the common ones include: Ragged Robin, Garlic Mustard, Red Campion, Cow Parsley (which is a major contributor to my annual suffering with hay-fever), Foxgloves, and another member of the Orchid family, the Broad-leaved Helleborine. This plant has solitary stems with pinkish-violet Orchid flowers and can be seen from July to September. The leaves are broad ending in a point and they are ribbed, clasping the stem, growing in a spiral formation up the stem.

There are over 400 species of plant in the Reserve and I can only mention a few of them, so there are many other plants to see throughout the year. Some that were familiar to me have not appeared in recent times, possibly due to changes in their required habitat, or changes to the light and shade in their chosen place. One such that I always enjoyed seeing was Butterbur because it was a bit unusual. It used to be over near the wooded area at the far side of the millpond, but that was back in February 2013. The strange pinkish flower heads, without ray florets, appear out of the bare ground in early spring, February-March, and the stout stem has pinkish scales. The rhubarb-like leaves appear later on and become really impressively large round, and toothed as they mature. They may still appear somewhere on the Reserve, but I haven't located any since 2013.

Image 58 The Broad-leaved Helleborine along the woodland path. Photo taken August 2016

INSECTS

In the meadow during July and August loads of Cinnabar Moth caterpillars can be seen all over the Ragwort plants. They are so easy to identify being bristly, coloured orange with black stripes and a black head. The colourful adult moths fly May to July and lay eggs on the underside of the Ragwort leaves. They only have one generation per year, and they sometimes fly during the daytime.

In the meadow are you might also see the Common Blue Butterfly, anytime between April and September as it has two or three broods per year. The male has blue upper wings but the female is usually brown. Its foodplants are the Trefoils, Vetches and Clovers.

Image 59 Cinnabar Moth Caterpillars. Photo taken July 2017

In the Butterfly Ride, which is a wide clearing through the woodland at the rear of the Reserve, on a good sunny summer's day you may see several species of butterfly, but one to look out for during June to August is the Silver-washed Fritillary. It is a lovely large, orange butterfly with a lovely pattern of spots and lines. It often may be found on Brambles or Thistles. The 'silver' aspect of the name is found on the underside of the wings which are greenish with some silver streaks. The female may lay her yellow, ridged egg on mosses on the shady side of a tree trunk.

The Speckled Wood is another species to find warming up on some sunlit vegetation. They are speckled, creamy-yellow on a dark brown background. Caterpillar food plants include grasses, in particular Couch-grass and Cock's-foot Grass. There are two, sometimes three, generations per year. These butterflies are commonly present from March to June, and July to September. They feed on aphid honeydew and Ragwort.

There have been about 33 species of Butterfly recorded at the Reserve, so there are many more that you could look out for that I have not mentioned here.

Damselflies and Dragonflies are a delight to be found particularly around the pond areas and hedgerows or the meadow. At the Reserve about 11 species of Damselfly and 15 species of Dragonfly have been recorded.

Early in the year about April you may see a Large Red Damselfly. It has black legs and the thorax is black with red stripes. It has clear wings with one black spot which it holds over its back when at rest. The females may be more yellow and darker generally. The eyes are separated and are red.

The Common Blue Damselfly is likely to be seen flying from May to September. The male is blue with black stripes on the thorax and has a black mark like a goblet on the 2nd segment of the blue and black abdomen. It also has one black spot on the clear wings. The females are usually green.

Images 60 & 61 Silver-washed Fritillary Butterfly, photo taken July 2017. Below, A Common Blue Butterfly in 2018

Images 62 & 63 Speckled Wood Butterfly, photo taken August 2013, and Below: Small Skipper, photo taken July 2017

Image 64 Small Copper, photo taken September 2018

Another insect I have seen along the boardwalk in autumn was a Common Darter Dragonfly and the abdomen of the male is an orange-red. The female's abdomen is more orange-brown. They fly from June until October.

By the Boldings Brook bridge I have often stopped to admire some attractive Beautiful Demoiselles. They look extra special in the sunshine due to their metallic blue-green colouring and red eyes. These are in the Damselfly family and may be seen during the main summer months.

A fairly large and distinct Dragonfly I have seen often in mid-summer is the Broad-bodied Chaser which has a wide flattened pale blue abdomen with yellow edges. The female has a yellow-brown abdomen.

Image 65 Common Blue Damselfly at WLNR. Photo taken at the end of July 2019

A brightly coloured Cardinal Beetle which had a scarlet head and wing case, black legs and antennae was basking in the sun on the delicate umbel flower of the Water Dropwort. It eats other smaller insects and when at the larval stage under tree bark the larvae feed also on other insect larvae. Another brightly coloured common insect is the Soldier Beetle, more well known as a Bloodsucker – named for its colour – but is quite harmless to us. Both of these insects are seen between May and August.

FAUNA

One time on the way back to the Visitor Centre I was excited to see a Grass Snake swimming in the Boldings Brook just a few metres away. I have also seen two more recently swimming across the millpond. They are really noticeable by their V-shape wake in the water.

Image 66 Common Darter Dragonfly. Photo taken in October 2017

Image 67 Broad-bodied Chaser. Photo taken in May 2017

Images 68 & 69 Marble Galls on Oak leaves caused by Gall Wasps. and (below) Willow Leaf Gall caused by a Sawfly

Marsh Frogs have a lime green stripe top to bottom of the body. In June their song can be heard which is a loud raucous noise like a bawdy laugh. In 2021 the millpond area near the field gate was deafening with the Marsh Frogs' noisy song. It is a kind of laughter that makes you want to join in! Non-native Marsh Frogs are larger than our native Common Frog. Apparently, they were released from a garden pond in Kent in 1935 and have been really successful and spread throughout the Home Counties since then. They make a tasty meal for hungry Herons, Egrets and Grass Snakes.

Staying with smaller animals, there are often Bank Voles to be seen near to the birdfeeders. They rush out grab some grains from the ground level and dash back to their hiding place. At the most recent feeding station at the back of the field I have seen the Voles emerge from the pile of logs as well as from the wooded area. They are very quick; so blink and you might miss them. In the 'Woodpecker Hide' feeding station they hide under wood or stumps and dive out and back so fast they can easily be unnoticed. Field Voles and Bank Voles may also be found in peoples' gardens. Their heads are more rounded and their ears less noticeable, but their tails are shorter than those of Mice.

Square-shaped Dormice 'tunnels' are attached to some trees near the rear of the Reserve. Dormice don't spend time on the ground but prefer to travel along low branches of trees. So, the square tunnel boxes have plasticine (or similar) on the floor base, and a Dormouse would walk through leaving footprints so that we then know they are present. Nesting boxes have all been placed in suitable locations. Dormice feed on flowers, fruit and hazel nuts. They are protected by law in this country.

I noticed a dead Mole at the Reserve very recently. It was in the middle of the upper path beyond the millpond. I stopped to marvel at its beautifully formed front claws, perfect for digging and moving earth. The black body fur has a velvety appearance. It has a pink snout with a specialized scent sensor in order to

Image 70 The Non-native Marsh Frogs are well established now in the Home Counties (2017)

Image 71 A Small Bank Vole in the centre of the picture. Photo taken February 2021

locate its prey. Moles eat earthworms and insect larvae. They are predated by Buzzards, Owls, and Stoats. Talking of predation by Owls reminds of a fun thing to do, and that is, to dissect and investigate an owl pellet should you find one. The results can be amazing: lots of very tiny bones that can be identified, perhaps with someone knowledgeable helping you. The bones could be from voles, mice, shrews and sometimes, a bat.

Foxes and Badgers are present on the Reserve, but they are seldom seen – just evidence of their presence. Sometimes there are footpad prints, sometimes dung or droppings. You may be lucky enough to see some Deer. Occasionally I have seen a few Deer together in the woodland on the upper path of the millpond. I have also seen some in the Walnut Tree Plantation woodland. I find photographing them too challenging with my small camera because as soon as they realise someone is around and watching them, they run off extremely quickly.

I seldom mention Grey Squirrels but there are many on the Reserve, but I personally consider them to be pests. Far more attractive are the native Red Squirrels, but of course we don't see them in Horsham.

FUNGI

Looking amongst the trees you usually can find various Fungi and different types of Lichens and Mosses. Some are very difficult to put a name to. When you really look around for fungi it is surprising how much you find and you realise there's so much to learn. When do they appear? What wood or ground are they on? All the differing shapes, colours, textures. gill arrangements, and so on. I often take pictures of fungi and then try to identify them later, usually with some assistance from some more knowledgeable people. Looking in books can make life difficult as often there is confusion with similarities in descriptions and then doubts as to what precisely you have found.

In 2017, I joined in with a 'Recorders' Challenge and on the February list was Yellow Brain Fungus. I thought I'd found some but it was actually Yellow Slime Mould instead. The great thing was that I had photographed the whole tree stump and there, below the slime, was some black pearl-like tiny balls which was, in fact another Slime Mould, much rarer named *Metatrichia floriformis*, which was a 'first' recording at the Reserve!

However, there are a few that can easily be identified and learned. One such is the Chicken-of-the-Woods, which is bright yellow and has orange zones on the upper surface. It can be high up a deciduous tree trunk or on tree stumps, with many thick overlapping irregular shaped brackets, edged with a sulphur yellow. It pales to white as it ages. It appears during the summer months.

Glistening Inkcaps can be found from May to November and they usually grow in clusters around old deciduous stumps, or over buried dead wood. They have flecks, or scales on the elongated egg-shaped cap, but those disappear with age. Inkcaps don't actually produce any inky fluid. They are common and widespread.

King Alfred's Cakes, or Cramp Balls are another common fungus to find at any time of the year, and they look similar to burnt cakes. It used to be believed that carrying some in your pockets prevent you from getting cramp. They begin reddish but change to black in a cluster of ball-like shapes and are found mostly on dead Ash or Birch wood. If cut through vertically, distinctive concentric black and white bands can be seen. Unlikely to be confused with any other fungus.

Beefsteak Fungus is red to red-brown and often found on Oak or Sweet Chestnut trunks during July to October. It can exude a red liquid and that is how it got its common name. It is a bracket fungus with a sandpapery texture on the upper surface, and the red turns brownish with age. It is widespread and fairly common.

Image 72 & 73 *Metatrichia floriformis* is a black lumpy Slime Mould. Photo taken February 2017. Below: Chicken-of-the-Woods. Photo taken May 2018

A fungus that is eye-catchingly scarlet is the small Scarlet Elf Cup and this can be found on dead wood and mosses in January to April. It has a short stem, but looks quite attractive though it has several other names in folklore: like Moss Cups and Fairy Baths.

Bay Polypore is a shallow convex funnel-shaped fungus, darker brown at the centre found on decayed wood or stumps of deciduous trees found during May to October. The example on the next page was in October 2018.

Jelly Ear Fungus can be found all year round on deciduous trees, particularly on Elder. Looking like a floppy ear when new but getting hard and brittle with age.

There are many fungi to be found on the Reserve, and a good many of them can be found in the Walnut Tree Plantation area. It is a pleasant wooded place to wander quietly along the paths and you might even see a few Deer as well. Also, there are plenty of bird boxes around the plantation. I have attended two 'Fungus Forays' at the Reserve in the past and have found them enjoyable and quite informative. All over the Reserve you will be able to see many different types of Fungus, Mosses and Lichens.

Image 74 Scarlet Elf Cup. Photo taken mid-March 2018

Amongst other fungi I have noticed are: The Common Stinkhorn, Dead Man's Fingers, and Candle Snuff Fungus. The unattractive and so-called Dog Vomit Fungus is actually a yellow foamy looking Slime-mould and not actually a fungus. It can appear on mulch in late spring, usually after heavy rain.

Images 75 & 76 Bay Polypore, Photo taken in October 2018 and Below: Jelly Ear Fungus from the Walnut Tree Plantation January 2006

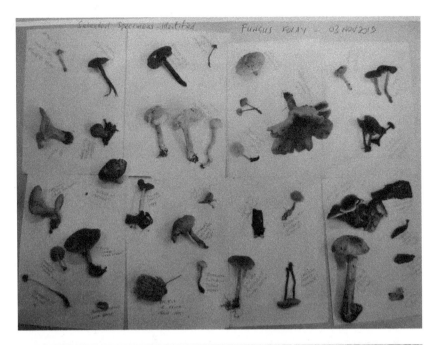

Images 77 & 78 The Results of a Fungus Foray 2019. Below:
Glistening Inkcaps. Photo taken in 2019

MOSSES

Images 79 & 80 Moss with fruiting bodies. Below: Moss with Dead Man's Fingers Fungus 2016

Image 81 Moss with parasitic scarlet fungus on a dead stump with Turkeytail Fungus. Photo taken March 2014

Image 82A A Flooded Area at the Reserve in March 2018, after a long period of rainy days

Image 82B British White Cattle in the Wet Meadow Area. Photo taken June 2015

CHAPTER FIVE

CHESWORTH FARM AREA
(Also listed in Green Spaces of Horsham 2013)

There are many fields and paths for walking at the Chesworth site (on the Eastern side of Horsham). Fields with wonderful names such as Jenny Barelegs and paths incorporating the lower part of Pedlars Way that ascends up hill (though not actually part of the Chesworth Farm and is about a seven mile walk all the way to

Image 83 Looking back towards Horsham town from up Jenny Barelegs field and Little Horsham Hill

Southwater) and part of the river Arun as far as Kerves Lane. The site covers about 90 acres. There are some special birds inhabiting the site which include Barn Owls, Skylarks, Yellowhammers, Whitethroats, and in the recently dedicated wetland area you may well see a Heron, some Swallows in the summer, and Damselflies and Dragonflies too. There are also a group of Pygmy goats, a pair of Llamas, British White Cattle, and the Hebridean and Herdwick sheep all keeping the grazing at specific times of the year.

I walk with friends most weeks on the Chesworth fields and paths. There are so many paths that you can always find somewhere 'new' to look for wildlife

BIRDS

Around Chesworth Farm there are many bird species to be seen. In 2007 there were records for at least 78 different species, so I have only written about some that I have particularly noticed. When walking along the lower riverside path behind the Tip-fields there is plenty of scruffy hedging for quite some distance and it is raised up from the path due to the topography of these fields. This is just the kind of unkempt hedge preferred by Whitethroats, and they nest quite low down in them during the summer period. They can be seen anytime from mid-April to early October when they migrate back to tropical Africa. They belong to the Warbler family and the male bird has a grey head, brown back with rusty wings and a white throat, but the female has a brown head brown back with rusty wings and a white throat. They eat insects and beetles till late summer when they eat berries before they migrate. Although I believe the Whitethroat is quite a common summer visitor, I have rarely caught sight of one. Their scratchy-phrased song can be frequently heard in the hedgerows.

I can't resist sharing with you my excitement at being invited in July 2010 to Chesworth to see some Barn Owls in action. At dusk the male flew to and from the meadow adjacent to the nest site and returned with voles or mice about every five minutes or so.

A bit later in the year, the young had been enticed out of the nest site and I saw them sitting on fence posts nearby, all in a row. There were five of them so there must have been a plentiful number of small mammals about during that season! Then the male fed the young waiting on the posts. I think the young ones would have flown off within a few days, as soon as they learned to predate their own meals. Still, it was such a wonderful thing to be there and watch them all.

In the recently made wetland area it is possible sometimes to see a Kestrel. There are plenty of tall trees for perches and a large area to find prey on the ground. They eat voles, insects, earthworms, as well as small birds. There is now a Kestrel box in the wetland area which I think was occupied this year (2021). They are a delight to watch as they hover above with their head into the wind and they glide down and drop on to their prey. They can also catch small birds in flight. In another field I have also seen a Common Buzzard make a kill and fly to a nearby Oak tree to eat its meal.

In the wet meadow area, I have in the past noticed a Grey Heron standing very still, probably hoping to eat a frog or two. I have occasionally seen some Swallows in the height of summer swooping low over the wettest part, gathering insects.

On a guided walk, in late summer a few years ago, whilst walking along a path in the middle of some adjacent fields, we could see a small flock of about twenty Meadow Pipits on the far side of the field. They were flitting round tufts of the grasses and then rose up and flew off again. It is also great to know that there are Skylarks on some of the Chesworth Farm fields, though it is vitally important not to disturb them, especially when they are nesting because they are ground-nesters. Dogs should always be kept on a lead particularly when near the Skylarks' field. Skylarks have become quite rare in many parts of the country.

In the both pond areas, before leaving the long drive (Plat Pond), and also in the wet meadow area, I have seen and heard Reed

Image 84 Canada Geese and Goslings. Photo taken in May 2021

Image 85 A Grey Heron at Chesworth. Photo taken September 2017

Warblers and seen a Moorhen with her chicks, which have red bills with a yellow tip, and black bodies. Both Moorhen parents help incubate the eggs and look after the chicks. Walking through to the wetland area at the bottom of Pedlars Way I saw two Canada Geese with six very small goslings.

There's another path that leads from the Plat Pond up to the Spring Barn and Wheat-rick fields. I have often used this path and always pleased if I have heard or caught sight of some Yellowhammers. These birds are in the Bunting family, so fairly small and the male is yellow and brown with a rusty colour on its rump, but the females are somewhat duller, with brown heads. A Yellowhammer's nest is made of straw and grass, lined with grass and hair, and usually built near the base of a hedge. The Yellowhammer sings pleasantly from the top of a hedge but adds a longer rasp-like sound before the end of a phrase. I think Yellowhammers are less abundant nowadays.

The Greenfinch is another bird that has suffered a loss of numbers lately and I think it may even be on the RSPB Red List, but as I mentioned in a previous chapter, they decreased rapidly due to a disease. I have still heard a few in recent years whilst walking around this area.

Blackcaps seem to be very abundant around Horsham, as wherever I go for a summer walk, I often hear them singing out their loud, distinctive and clear song. The male has the black cap but the female has a brown cap. They used to be only a summer visitor but now it is quite possible to see them during the winter months as well. They make a fragile twig and grass nest in low bushes or brambles.

I observed the group of British White Cattle in the Tip field and was surprised to notice these five members of the Crow family perched on the back of the one that was standing up.

Image 86 The Arun, Pedlars Way. Photo taken on a sunny day in October 2017

Image 87 Corvids on the (standing) British White Cattle's Back at Chesworth March 2017

FLOWERS

Flowers in the wetland area in May include Yellow Rattle, Greater Stitchwort and Red Campion to name just a few. There are also many different types of Grasses such as Yorkshire Fog and Rice Grass, Timothy Grass, Cock's-foot Grass. Sow Thistles and Spear Thistles are present, too. There are some plants in the wettest places like Yellow Flag Iris, Branched Bur-reed, Common Reed and Water Mint.

Yellow Rattle was mentioned in detail earlier, though it is an important plant to help establish flower meadows.

Greater Stitchwort is a very common flower that can be seen from March till June and grows in a patch among grass and other flowers along hedgerows. The five white petals are cleft centrally and the pale leaves are narrow and lanceolate. Lesser Stitchwort is smaller but similar in appearance (but the petals are divided nearly to the base) and these can be seen from May to August.

Red Campion can grow to two or three feet high. It can be seen from March to November and flowers continuously with pinkish-red flowers and downy stems. It has brown seed pods when ripe, and this plant can spread rapidly.

Common Knapweed is easily recognisable by its solitary pinkish-purple flower heads with dark scale-like bracts. This flowers from June to September and has pointed spear-like leaves and a stiff stem.

One summer I found Tall Melilot near one of the gates between fields. It is a member of the pea family and flowers from May to September with long, golden yellow clusters of pea-like flowers. It has trefoil leaves which are toothed.

In a recently led walk in an area where people are not usually permitted, a rarer tiny Vetch was noted, (*Vicia hirsuita*), as well as an Orchid or two.

Water Mint has a pleasant scent. The flowers are pale lilac and rounded with hairy sepals and oval pointed leaves. This flowers from July to October and is likely to hybridise with other mints in the damp area.

A recent project at the rear of the Volunteer Centre is a wildlife garden project. This garden has a few fruit trees, nettles, thistles and grasses. Additionally, there is an uncommon Clary, and this is a hairy perennial with violet-blue flowers held in whorls of 4-6 narrow spires and flowering in June and July. The upper leaves are stalkless but the basal leaves are ovate, double-tooth and stalked. This plant is common in Europe, but rarer in Southern England.

Image 88 The Clary in the Wildlife Garden. Photo taken in June 2022

Image 89 Tall Melilot near a field gate, Chesworth. Photo taken July 2016

INSECTS

One lovely sunny summer morning in 2017, I was with a group of walkers along a footpath by the side of some fields. The grasses were being cut for hay and the cutting machinery left it in rows of 'grass ridges'. We became aware of a cloud of fluttering butterflies, following along after the tractor. They were all Meadow Browns – I don't think I've ever seen so many together before – I stopped counting them after I'd got to seventy, but there were many more than that. The Meadow Brown is common in grassy areas and flies from June until August. The female is larger than the male and also has a larger orange patch with an eyespot on the forewing, where the male has smaller orange patch and eyespot. The larger, darker eyespot of the female is noticeable on the underside of the wings, too.

The Speckled Wood may very often be found sunning itself usually in a patch of sunshine on a woodland path or vegetation. On the forewings, the female has more yellow scales around the eyespot than the males. It is double-brooded and the larva is green and feeds on grasses. Rival males may be seen spiralling in aerial battles. The Speckled Wood is unusual in that it can overwinter as a pupa or as a larva.

I have described the Orange-tip, which flies during April to June in more detail in an earlier chapter. The first sighting of this butterfly epitomises spring to me.

Around the wetland meadow you may often see Dragonflies and Damselflies between the months of April and September time, and in October if the weather is mild. Some of the insects I have seen there include the Four-spotted Chaser which has a brown-amber body, with amber triangles at the base of the hind wings, and a spot on the front edge of each wing. This sighting was on an 'Insect Walk' in May 2018.

Also in the same family, a Broad-bodied Chaser where the mature male has a blue abdomen with yellow spots along the sides. A large fast-flying Hawker is the Emperor Dragonfly, where the male has a light green thorax and a blue abdomen with a black line all down it. The female is similar but has a greenish-blue abdomen.

Another red dragonfly is the medium-sized Ruddy Darter. This has black legs, a bright red abdomen in the male, but the female is an ochre colour.

Additionally, I have seen the Large Red Damselfly which has black legs and red stripes on the thorax (unlike the Small Red Damselfly which has red legs and no stripes on the thorax).

The Common Blue Damselfly, which has different marking on the second abdominal segment from other blue members of this Family. It may also be seen in grassland and woodland when away from breeding sites.

A common Hoverfly to be seen throughout the year is the Marmalade Fly, which is smaller than some others, but mimics a wasp's colouring pattern (although more orange than yellow). It is often noticed in parks, woodlands and gardens. and the adults live about twelve days feeding on nectar, although I have also read that, unusually, they have the ability to crush and eat pollen. The larvae are very small worm-like and legless and are nocturnal predators of aphids.

Image 90 Four-spotted Chaser, Chesworth. Photo taken in May 2018

Image 91 A Ruddy Darter Dragonfly, Chesworth. Photo taken in September 2016

Roesel's Bush Cricket used to only be found in the South East region, but in recent years it has extended its range North and West through grassland corridors. It needs these and damp meadows. The bush cricket is dark brown with orange legs, green face and has two to three cream spots on thorax.

In the new wildlife garden, there was a patch of tall thistles. On the day I visited, there were lots of Ladybirds near the tops of the plants and also some freshly laid yellow ladybird eggs. They were all Harlequin Ladybirds which are non-native to the UK. There was one with black elytra and two large red spots, and the ones pictured with orange elytra and many black spots.

Images 92 & 93 Two Harlequin Ladybirds on the Thistles, and (Below) Ladybird eggs Photos taken in June 2022

Image 94 The Wetland Area, Chesworth. Photo taken one damp day in January 2017

FAUNA

The Common Frog is a greenish-brown colour with darker blotches on the skin. Spawning takes place around March time. When the tadpoles have transformed into very small frogs, they may be found hopping around in the wet meadow area.

The Grass Funnel-weaver Spider makes a sheet web in grasses and low shrubs. It is olive-grey in colour with a chevron pattern on the abdomen and three pale bands on the brown carapace. From this sheet there is a funnel-like tube of webbing where the spider waits for her prey to get trapped on the sheet and the spider can then rush out and drag it back to its retreat. The adults are seen between June and August.

There are 18 species of Bats found in the UK. There are also a few species of Bat living around Chesworth. Bats are flying mammals. The usual bat to notice over wetlands after dusk is the Daubenton's Bat which has short ears and flies over water snatching insects from the surface. They may live in open woodland in a hole in a tree, or under bridges or tunnels. They hibernate underground over the winter months.

In some fields there are places you may find lots of mole hills, but you would be very fortunate to actually see a Mole.

Field and Bank Voles are among the mammals listed in the Chesworth Farm Management Plan (2007). I haven't seen them myself though I haven't been out looking for signs that would tell me they are there. I expect that Voles could be also be present in the new wildlife garden as various favourable habitats will exist there, too. The Wood Mouse as well is likely to put in an appearance as well since there are bird feeders and good cover for small mammal homes.

Foxes, Rabbits, Hedgehogs, Weasels and Shrews are also present on the farmland.

FUNGI

In November 2021 I joined a small group of people on a Fungus walk, led by Jonathan Simons. We found a good variety of fungi starting at the rear of the Volunteer Centre: Common Bonnet, Purplepore Bracket, and Turkeytail Fungus, on some wood and woodpiles.

Turkeytail has semi-circular brackets with thin wavy margins. It dries hard and keeps its colour for a long time. It forms many rows in overlapping tiers on dead stumps and logs. It may be seen throughout the year and is very common.

Image 95 Turkeytail Fungus is a multi-coloured bracket fungus. Photo taken November 2021

A Giant Puffball, was found along the path to the Backfield, with some Mottlegills, found in the grass. On a mossy log there were some small fungi poking through that were white with black tops, looking like matchsticks. King Alfred's Cakes were seen on a dying Ash tree trunk along the pathway and a group of Sulphur Tuft Fungus, was found on a dead wood log. In a triangle between pathways, we saw Candle Snuff Fungus and Angel's Bonnet Fungus which is bell-shaped.

Candle Snuff Fungus is also found on deadwood and logs at any time of year. The stalk is black and the upper part white, almost like snuffed out candle wicks. Along the main drive there was a Deceiver and a Webcap under some Oaks and the hedgerow. Fairy- Ring Mushrooms were found in the grass along the main drive and a Yellowing Knight fungus was found at the base of a fencepost near the Oaks. This was a significant number of finds within a short distance of the Volunteer Centre, so quite a good result.

Image 96 Giant Puffball Fungus in the Backfield. November 2021

The Giant Puffball can be very large – around 50 cm across and also weighs a lot. It grows in grassy places especially if it is nitrogen rich soil and it can grow on compost heaps. The season for this large fungus is from summer into autumn.

Pixie Cup Lichen has funnel-like cups, The stalks taper towards the bottom, and have a granulated texture. It grows on decomposing wood and also on heaths.

Image 97 Common Bonnets. November 2021

Image 98 Candle Snuff Fungus. November 2021

Image 99 Pixie Cup Lichen along the fence line of Plat's Pond.
November 2021

Image 100 Not wild animals, but part of the Chesworth landscape
nowadays, are the two female Llamas which are very good at defending
other livestock from predators. Photo taken February 2021

Image 101 Chesworth Wetland Scene painted by the author and presented to the Friends of Chesworth Farm 2017

CHAPTER SIX

KNEPP CASTLE ESTATE, NEAR SHIPLEY. SOUTH OF HORSHAM AT SMALL DOLE

Image 102 The current Knepp Castle. Photo taken 2005

The original moated Norman Knepp Castle ruins may be seen from the roadside from the A24. It was later used as a hunting lodge and then finally destroyed during the English Civil War in the mid-1600's. The Knepp Estate is owned by Sir Charles and Lady Burrell. The Estate covers about three and a half thousand acres, with a large area around the present Castle kept as gardens and a Deer Park. The majority of the land was used for arable farming until about twenty years ago. The Knepp Estate has often featured in the news recently as a successful example of a re-wilding project. What led the Burrells to abandon farming and to attempt this scheme?

Sir Charles conceived the idea around the turn of the century after concluding the farm as it was could never be profitable on such heavy clay and so he sold up his herds and machinery. The idea was to establish a biodiverse wilderness instead.

Re-wilding does not mean letting the land go wild and unkempt: restoring things to recover nature, creating different habitats still requires planned management. Lady Burrell, (Isabella Tree), has written a comprehensive book (*Wilding*, first published in 2018) explaining and setting out all the steps that have been taken during the wilding process.

By 2003 the Southern Block of the Knepp Estate was left fallow. Generally, farming practices destroy habitats and drives out wildlife, but to allow them to return in the newly created habitats, the restoration requires a variety of grazing animals that graze in differing ways. This then allows different trees and plant habitats to grow specifically suiting birds, plants and insects that had previously vanished from that area. Restoration of habitat has also taken place along the river Adur including the creation of scrapes in a flood plain.

I first went to tour and see the grounds circa 2005 with a local Natural History Society. We were shown round by Sir Charles, and at that time the Burrells had recently embarked on their extensive programme to re-wild the majority of the Estate in three sections, which started with the Southern Block. The Northern and Middle Blocks were later brought in to the scheme. Farming here had not been profitable and so after researching wilding processes, it was decided to turn areas of the Estate over for that purpose. The natural history that has evolved over the last

15–20 years has been nothing short of amazing and a great eye-opener to us all. Of course, from another viewpoint, conservation is also involved here. Animals used for different reasons in the re-wilding process have been Exmoor Ponies, Tamworth Pigs, English Longhorn Cattle, Fallow Deer, Red Deer, and various breeds of Sheep.

By 2018, DEFRA's 25-year environment plan had named Knepp as an outstanding example of landscape restoration in recovering nature.

BIRDS

Too numerous to mention all the bird species now present, but there have been some extra special birds that have found the wild Knepp now provides ideal habitats for them to flourish.

When I first visited early in this project, I was with a group and we were shown a sawn through piece of tree trunk with a clear view of a typical Woodpeckers' nest. It was quite a surprise to me that the shape of nesting hole was angular and adapted to keep the chicks warm and safe. The entrance hole is about two inches round. The Woodpecker bores horizontally at first and then straight down. After laying eggs both parents incubate them for about two weeks. The chicks are helpless and have closed eyes for twelve days. They are fed on insects, tree seeds and other birds' eggs and they fledge in about three weeks.

Turtle Doves were first recorded at Knepp in 2007 and after that some Ravens, breeding Skylarks, Woodlarks, Jack Snipe, Redwings, Fieldfares, and Lesser Redpolls. Nightingales have also found territories there. In 2017 Peregrine Falcons have nested and in 2018 the first White Stork was recorded, too. The first Stork hatchling was noted in 2020, followed by about six Stork nests in 2021 all within Knepp's boundaries. All five species of UK Owls are to be found on the Estate, too. A selection of birds from the Red and Amber Lists have now relocated to Knepp.

I revisited the Southern part of Knepp in May 2021 on a pleasant morning walking 4.5km. There had been several items in newspapers and on television regarding the success of breeding Storks at Knepp now the rewilding has progressed to provide great habitats for them over the past few years. Near to the campsite and the farm shop there was a White Stork's nest at the top of a large tree. When I did my walk, there were young in the nest with one parent watching over them, waiting for a visit from the other parent to return with food for the young and to change over 'young-minding' duties. The first parent then flew away over the

Image 103 The tree trunk section shows the Woodpecker's nest excavation. Photo taken circa August 2005

fields to find more food. Another mile or so on there was another Stork nest in an Oak tree and that had three young in it.

Continuing my walk on footpaths along hedgerows at the edges of adjacent fields there was so much birdsong. I identified Blackcaps, Nightingales and many other songbirds, plus excitingly, I also heard the Cuckoo several times during the morning. It has been some years since I last heard Cuckoos. Later in the walk I saw a Whitethroat, and also heard a Lesser Whitethroat in the hedges and brambles.

It was also good to know that Turtle Doves were close-by on this walk as they have been so low on numbers in recent years. Turtles Doves are a much-endangered species and exist on only a few Sussex sites, Knepp included.

Image 104 The White Storks at Knepp. Photo taken May 2020

I believe a Hoopoe, Golden Oriole and Great White Egret were seen in 2020. Also, there were a few other rarer birds of prey residing on the Knepp Estate.

I don't know a great deal about White Storks. It has been a long time since individual birds were occasionally seen in the South of the UK until recently, when they established at Knepp, as mentioned before. I believe they do not breed until they are between three and seven years old. Three to five eggs may be laid and hatch in thirty days. Their nests are very large pile of sticks. Their courtship displays include bill rattling with their heads back, and ritualised bowing with wings spread out. They feed on frogs, voles, beetles and grasshoppers. Storks usually migrate away in September and return in March.

The Nightingale is often difficult to actually see and identify because it skulks around in undergrowth in dense hedges and bushes, but when you do see one the eye looks dark with a fine white line around it, and it has a rusty-coloured tail. The Nightingale's distinctive song is better known (and learned) as you are more often likely to discover their presence by listening, usually from April into May. They eat beetles, ants, worms and berries from the ground, especially in shaded areas. They nest on or near the ground building cups of leaves and grasses. They migrate to Africa in September.

FLOWERS

As you might expect, there are now some rare plants on the Estate which include, Adder's-tongue Fern, Marsh Speedwell and the Water Violet. Adder's-tongue Fern is an unusual fern which has a short stem up to 30cm, and a single stalk that bears the spores which ripen from June to August. It grows in grasslands or meadows. Marsh Speedwell which is only 15 cm, and has whitish flowers tinged with blue from June to August and grows in wet meadows on acid soil. Water Violet is an aquatic plant with a flower spike above water seen in May to June. The flowers are not violet, but lilac-pink with a yellow throat, and the leaves are submerged.

There are far too many plants to name and comment about so I have picked out just a few. The Carline Thistle grows on lime grassland. They have stiff stems up to 60cm. The flowers are brownish yellow seen from July to September, though dead plants in winter still look much the same. They are biennial plants.

The Dog Rose is a common wild rose which blooms in June to July. There are five pink or white petals that are slightly fragrant. Later, the egg-shaped hips ripen to a bright red. It typically grows in area of scrub. The Bramble, also part of the scrublands, is dense and prickly but of great benefit to the small birds which nest in it, like the Wren and Whitethroats and a few others. Brambles also form a barrier around sapling trees giving them early protection from browsing animals. The blackberries are a vital food source for many creatures in the autumn.

Ivy is another plant worth mentioning as it has many benefits to insects and birds. In spring Wrens and Robins may nest in the dense foliage. In September when the Ivy flowers it provides late nectar for Butterflies, Queen Bumblebees, Wasps and Hoverflies. The leaves are also food for the larvae of the Holly Blue Butterfly and the Swallowtail Moth and later on becomes good place for the Brimstone and Comma Butterflies to hibernate. Some birds shelter or roost in the leaves like Sparrow or Starlings. The black Ivy berries are winter food for Thrushes.

In one field I noticed a large circle of Silverweed with its yellow flowers and silvery pinnate leaves. It is a low, prostrate but pretty plant that spreads with runners. It flowers from May to August.

Although there are many other plants are on the Estate in all the differing habitats, I have yet to go on a plant 'hunt' and suggest you visit and see what you can spot. When I returned to my car in the small car park near to the campsite area, I noticed a whole

125

bank of Red and some White Campions for several yards down the drive.

There are so many different trees species at Knepp but only two that I will mention here. There are some especially ancient Oak trees, particularly on the land nearer the present Castle, (the Midblock), and many other Oaks all around the Estate.

Ash die-back has caused a problem in the UK since 2012 and now it has spread across the country. So, like any other deciduous woods, at Knepp they, too, have the Ash die-back problem. Many of dead Ash trees have had to be felled. It is hoped to find a resistant Ash that will be able to provide saplings resistant to

Image 105 An Old Tree. Photo taken on a visit in the early 2000s

this disease, so that in time, the dead Ash trees can be successfully replaced.

INSECTS

Butterflies: several rarer species have been recorded and in 2015 the UK's largest breeding population of Purple Emperor Butterflies was on the Knepp Estate. I regret to say that at this moment of writing I know very little about this particular butterfly, though I am aware that most of its time is spent in the tree tops making it difficult for an undiscerning eye to observe. I believe it does spend some time on the ground, especially if lured down with such delightful bait as 'dog poo' or other animal droppings. The male has the flashy purple sheen on its wings when seen in bright light. They fly in June and July. The larva is green and shaped rather like a rolled leaf which, again, makes it difficult to notice. It feeds on Goat Willow.

The Large Tortoiseshell was quite common in the UK when I was a child, but numbers have dwindled since and it was thought to be extinct for many decades. While occasionally a small number have been seen in coastal areas of Dorset and East Sussex over the years, they were from overseas and not breeding here. Males and females of the Large Tortoiseshell have been found this year on the Knepp Estate where there is the right scrubland habitat now. (According to a newspaper article I read on the 9th June 2022).

Around 2016, some rare invertebrates had been recorded and 62 species of Bees, 30 species of Wasps, many Beetles, Moths and Micro-moths.

FAUNA

It was lovely to see the British Longhorn Cattle grazing in one of the fields. Their horns really are very long. They are a tough breed that look after themselves all year round, in all sorts of weather. In another area there was a large Tamworth Pig with some sizeable piglets – their ginger coats shining in the sunlight. The Tamworths were chosen for Knepp because they disturb the land in a similar way to Wild Boars, but Tamworths are not aggressive like the Boars, which makes it safer for the public walking through the footpaths on the Estate. Further along the footpath I came across several Exmoor Ponies on the penultimate leg of the walk. They also are a tough breed used to whatever weather is thrown at them. One the delights of the morning was when suddenly a group of Roe Deer shot out of a wooded area on my left, across the field and through to another field on the other side of a hedged area.

The different animals used to graze on the Estate are there because the animals graze in diverse ways. For example, as mentioned above, the magnificent Tamworth Pigs effectively plough the land as they root around the ground searching for nuts, roots or bulbs or even worms. When the Deer graze, they create a different height of browse line than the Cattle. The Cattle sometimes browse on Sallow. as well as grass. Exmoor Ponies munch grassland, and the Rabbits create a very low browse line. These different ways of grazing help to create different landscape habitats evolve by allowing diverse plants, trees, grass and scrub to develop. Of course, I saw many rabbits during the morning and evidence of warrens all over the place.

A couple of years ago, a pair of Beavers was released at Knepp recently, but I believe one of them escaped, so it was an experiment that did not go to plan at that time. (See also Appendix 2)

The Bat species present at Knepp include most of the species that can be found in the UK which is very good news, though I haven't ever looked for them as they appear after dusk to feed on moths, midges, beetles and flies. (All UK Bats feed on insects. Some bats in other countries feed on fruit and other prey – I have seen many Fruit Bats in Sydney, Australia).

I did notice a Common Toad in the wet meadows one time, though toads are more likely to be seen at night time. They live mostly in damp wood piles or leaf litter in shaded, moist places,

Image 106 An Oak with a Stork's nest and Deer racing across the field. Photo taken 2021

including woodland. They feed mainly on earthworms, insects and slugs. The females are larger than the males. They vary in colour from brown to green or grey and have 'warty' skin. If threatened Toads secrete a vile-tasting substance to defend itself against predators. A Toad has copper-coloured eyes with a horizontal pupil. Toads walk or crawl unlike frogs that hop. Females lay spawn in long strings of tadpoles, which develop differently from frog tadpoles. Grass Snakes, Slow-worms and Lizards can also be found on the Estate.

FUNGI

During my first visit to Knepp, around 2005, there was excitement about the discovery of a rare Fungus, *Phellinus robustus*. It was on an old Oak in the Middle-block area named Repton Park. A few years later the same rare fungus was also found on an old

Image 107 The rare Fungus, *Phellinus robustus*

Oak in the Southern Block. By the size of the brackets, it had obviously been present for many years. It is possible that it has only been found in two other sites in the UK (as at 2011).

This successful wilding at Knepp shows that natural species will return, but it is necessary that the Knepp Estate is not just a 'nature island' and that connections can be made all over the countryside for species to thrive in the long term. We know it is good for our mental health to be outside with nature around us – this was particularly apparent during recent Covid lockdowns. My hope is that this small book by an amateur naturalist, will inspire readers to get up and out there observing nature for themselves!

Images 108 & 109 Longhorn Cattle. Below: A Longhorn

ADDENDUM
NEW HOUSE SIGHTINGS

At the end of November 2019, I moved to a house close to the northern boundary of the Horsham Park. It is really good position to discover more about the natural wildlife inhabiting the Park – but that will take time to achieve and I look forward to it. My time here has encompassed the whole of the Covid pandemic years, so I have had time to observe wildlife from the rear patio garden on the edge of the Park and around the Silver Birch tree and very large old Oak tree in the front of the property.

2020 – An Unusual Year

I decided to move house within Horsham in 2019 and eventually settled in to my new house a few weeks before Christmas in that year. I was now the owner of a courtyard in place of my previously significant area of garden, but my joy was that I was on the perimeter of the large Horsham Park. (56 acres).

So, during the Covid year of 2020, I had the added interest of watching birds that actually visited the courtyard regularly as well as some of the birds in the Park's tall trees beyond my fence line. These birds were Dunnocks, a pair of Blackbirds, a pair of Robins, Blue Tits, Great Tits, Coal Tits. Nuthatch, Magpies, Crows, a Tawny Owl, some Woodpigeons, a pair of Wrens, Greater Spotted Woodpecker, Green Finch, small flock of Long-tailed Tits, Chiffchaff and Blackcap in April, and a small group of Redwings in December 2020. Additional birds were a Jay I noticed in May and a Treecreeper and Pied Wagtail in June. There was more variety of bird species than I had at my previous address with the larger garden.

Image 110 The courtyard with tall Horsham Park trees behind. Photo August 2021

The Tawny Owl left a clear dusty print of itself on my bedroom window. It was totally identifiable, and fortunately it did not hit hard enough to cause itself any lasting harm. I often hear a Tawny Owl in the middle of the night. The visiting Redwings ate all the holly berries on the tree I have in full sight from my kitchen, and it was fun to watch them. They methodically ate the berries from the top of the tree down choosing a bit further down each day until the berries were all gone. Then they moved off to a new feeding site.

The delightful pair of tiny Wrens visited all my shrubs looking for tasty insects and spiders. They are so small but perfectly formed, and of course, the male has a really loud voice. I heard his lovely song most days in the spring, and other times of the year.

In February Blue Tits (as well as squirrels) have been obtaining some nectar from my Camellia flowers. It's a wonder I ever get to see the early blooms from this Camellia. I have also spotted the Blue Tits pecking away at the 'insect house' sealed bits of bamboo in order to grab an insect from there! Really early in the year, I've heard a Spotted Woodpecker drumming on a high branch in the huge nearby Oak at the end of the cul-de-sac and sometimes as well drumming on the Park trees behind my house.

I don't feed the birds but I have provided a birdbath in the courtyard, that has given me some great entertainment throughout the day. The female Blackbird is usually first for a wash about breakfast time, followed by the Blue Tits and Great Tits later in the morning and then the male Blackbird. In the afternoon a pair of Woodpigeons come down to drink and occasionally sit in the bath displacing all the water, so I have to refill it. Usually the Robins bathe in the late afternoon. Recently, I saw a Magpie in the birdbath.

I don't have any wild flowers here, except perhaps the Honeysuckle which grows out of hand sometimes along my fence. I do have some herbs and other plants to attract various bees, butterflies and hoverflies.

A very large Bumblebee, a Bee-fly and Honeybees were on the flowers in March. I noticed two Ladybirds: one was black with two red spots and the other was orange with 22 black spots. I think they were both Harlequin Ladybirds.

Butterflies I saw in April included: a Brimstone male and a female, Orange-tip, Red Admiral and a Common Blue. In June I saw a Cinnabar Moth which often fly in the daytime, and a Cabbage Moth (which is mottled brown tinged reddish with some white markings). I found another Mint Moth in the courtyard on my herbs.

A small Red Damselfly was seen in April as well as another that was red with two buff segments near the end of the abdomen, and a spot on each wing.

Very early in my first year here, there were about nine Grey Squirrels visiting the courtyard regularly, who were far too mischievous, eating the Camellia flowers and other young plant growth when their natural food supply was short, and also digging up and eating bulbs, and burying acorns from the Oak. Woodpigeons also stripped new growth off the Honeysuckle along my fence.

I have had other issues with the Grey Squirrels since I came to this property. They eat my freshly planted Daffodil and Tulip bulbs. They even perched on my fence and showed me that's what they were eating! When I used to feed the birds, I bought new bird feeders. I put inverted collars around the poles, but the squirrels then jumped from the fence height in order to steal the bird food. I then tried a particularly 'swinging' bird feeder on a hook near to the kitchen window and the squirrels really struggled to climb facedown the fence amongst rose bushes. Sometimes they over-balanced and tumbled down. Late, one tried hanging on to the swinging feeder and frequently panicked and lost balance. The antics were so funny I took a video one day. One squirrel came up the top of the fence panel and looked directly at me with half-closed eyes. Then it tried again to steal some food from the moving feeder. After many attempts it got back on top of the fence and gave me a really long hard stare! I found these antics most amusing. For the last two years, I stopped feeding the birds as it just encouraged rats from the Park to scrounge any food from the floor underneath the feeders. I found a Wood Mouse residing in the shed in mid-winter. I'm glad it had some shelter in the coldest months.

I have often heard foxes in the dead of night, especially in November when they begin their mating season. I have also seen them wandering in front of the houses. A few months ago, to my surprise, a neighbour told me that a Badger ran along in front of the houses and then disappeared into the Park.

A FEW OTHER LOCAL PLACES
TO GO AND SEE SOME NATURE

PULBOROUGH BROOKS
SOUTHWATER COUNTRY PARK
ST. LEONARDS FOREST

PULBOROUGH BROOKS
Only a few miles South of Horsham

Image 111 View from outside the Shop/Centre as you enter the Pulborough Brooks Reserve

It is well worth visiting Pulborough Brooks, particularly if you enjoy birdwatching. Of course, there is plenty of other nature present there if you look for it. The Pulborough Brooks site is only twenty-five minutes by car from Horsham. There are main paths to follow and several hides and different habitats. It is a place where you can learn more about birds as many knowledgeable people go there and like to share information, especially so if there happens to be an unexpected visiting bird. For example, on a recent trip (late February 2017) I was made aware that a Temminck's Stint was feeding within sight. It was certainly good to see it because it is a rare visitor that is also on the Vulnerable List. This Temminck's Stint differs in appearance from the Little Stint by way of being greyer and less marked on its back, it has

137

yellow legs and a darker breast, I learned. The Little Stint has a scaly pattern on its back, a white breast and black legs. They are both small, sparrow-sized waders and probe about for Insects and small invertebrates in the muddy margins of pools. Both these Stints are passage migrants, only seen very rarely in winter in Sussex. The Little Stint breeds in the Arctic tundra and Temminck's Stint in Scandinavia. I am fortunate to have seen the latter and to have had the opportunity to learn just a little about it.

There is a walk with scrub and hedges that Adders frequent in early spring when male emerge and bask in the sunshine. Female Adders emerge a bit later on. I have only once seen an Adder there, but I don't go looking for them.

Pulborough Brooks is also a great place to hear, and probably see, Nightingales during April and May. I was lucky to have seen one which flew to a perch on an exposed branch above the hedge line a few years back. I have also been fortunate enough to not only hear a Cuckoo, but to have seen it fly from trees on my left to another on the right in an area overlooking the Brooks and a distant view.

I have also witnessed a group of Nightjars late one evening in a wooded area near to the car park. They hide on the ground or in leaves, really well-camouflaged during the day and they are active nocturnally, thus they may appear in a clearing about three quarters of an hour after dusk. They feed on moths and flying beetles. They make an interesting and unusual rasp-like 'churring' sound. They are summer visitors and return to Africa in winter.

Some of the birds I have seen at Pulborough Brooks are the Kestrel, Red Kite, several Lapwings and Snipe. When a Red Kite appeared, all the ducks flocked and took flight together rising and falling to evade the Kite till the danger was over. Pochards, Pintails, Shovelers, Teals and Wigeon were on one of the ponds. In other habitats some Wrens, Robins, and Great Tits, Thrush and the 'dazzlingly dressed' male Pheasant, were all seen on a clear, cold but sunny February day. On another occasion in winter a fairly large number of Lapwings and some Snipe, were on an island and in one of the ponds. I have also seen Lapwings there in spring time. They have a noticeable crest, and their feathers have a lovely colourful metallic sheen in sunlight. In spring, the males fly up and tumble down 'uncontrollably' and then rise up again loudly beating their wings, which was interesting to witness. They nest in a scrape and will use distraction tactics if threatened. Their call is a 'pee-wit' sound which is how they got their old common name of 'Peewit'.

The Common Snipe needs damp, soft ground and tussocks of grass as ideal habitat, but unfortunately there are only a few suitable places for them in the countryside now, so more nest in Reserves. They often sit very still and are difficult to actually see due to their excellent camouflage feather patterns. They have a harsh rasping call if disturbed.

In summer time there are many butterflies and insects to see. I have seen all of the commonest butterflies there on wild flowers. I was

Image 112 Lapwing (top left) and Common Snipe (bottom right). Photo February 2018

Image 113 Skippers on Thistles, Pulborough Brooks 2017

pleased to find two Small Skippers in a Thistle patch. The Small Skipper is identified by its antennae which are orange at the tip, whereas the Essex Skipper has black tips to the antennae. Both Skippers hold their fore and hind wings on a different plane, so not like the usual way you see butterfly wings open or distinctly closed.

I have noticed plenty of rabbits at Pulborough Brooks often near to hedgerows on the field side areas. Rabbits are fairly commonly seen nowadays, but way back in my childhood around 1953, they suffered badly with *Myxomatosis* which decreased the wild rabbit population massively. I believe the disease was spread by biting insects. the male Rabbit is known as a buck, the female as a doe, and the young as kits or kittens. It is well known they can produce young many times in a year. They were introduced into Britain in the 12th century by the Normans.

On one visit, I noticed a group of four Grey Squirrels that appeared to be playing 'chase' for a considerable time on the edge

Image 114 Some Deer resting near one of the hides. Photo April 2013

Image 115 View across the Brooks. Photo 2018

of a woodland, near one of the hides. Since 2016 they have been listed as an invasive alien species of concern. They have spread widely and our native Red Squirrel in the UK has been almost knocked out, and only exists in some isolated places: for example, Brownsea Island, Scotland, and I have seen Red Squirrels on Tresco, in the Isles of Scilly.

SOUTHWATER COUNTRY PARK
(Close to Horsham)

Image 116   The Cripplegate Lake, near the Visitor Centre and Café. Photo 2020.

This site is 85 acres that was once a Brickworks. There are three lakes, grassland and woodland and it extends over the road from the main car park. There is plenty of wild life and plants to be seen, including a large number of Orchids in the grassland areas.

Mute Swans are present all year through, and there are Tufted Ducks, Coots and Moorhens. Occasionally you might see a Kingfisher, and there are Pied Wagtails and Reed Warblers.

The Common Spotted Orchid is abundant in the grasses to the left of the big lake and some more over the road in Ben's field, where I have also seen Adder's-tongue, a small arum-like plant. This is also where I have seen Grass Vetchling which is the only

Image 117   Spindle fruits by the Lake. Photo November 2020

pea-flower which has grass-like narrow leaves so it is difficult to find in grassland unless it is in flower, and it has no tendrils. The flowers in May to July are crimson-red. There is also a Bee Orchid near the smaller lake.

There are many Damselflies: Common Blue, a Blue-tailed, the White-legged and a Small Red. I've seen some Darter Dragonflies as well. Many species of Butterfly are present, too.

This shrubby Spindle was in the hedge. It has insignificant flowers around May or June, with four greenish yellow small petals. The noticeable bright seed cases expose a vivid orange fruit when ripe. The wood of a Spindle tree was used for making spindles for the wool trade.

ST. LEONARDS FOREST
(Horsham)

This forest area has much in the way of local history and myths as well as a bountiful mix of natural history. Natural history surveys have been carried out in the past which revealed long lists of Flora, Fungi, Birds, Butterflies and Moths, Mammals, and Fish.

Nowadays the forest covers about twelve square miles in which different habitats can be found: heathland, broadleaf and coniferous woodlands, and includes the Leechpool and Owlbeech areas, local to Horsham.

A few years ago, I went from the Roosthole car park, with a Natural History group on a guided walk. Among the special sightings we encountered were two Adders, two Grass Snakes and a Slow-worm – the latter looking snake-like but is in fact a legless

Image 118   A Slow-worm. Photo taken in the early 2000s

lizard. The highlight of this walk was waiting around after dusk for the secretive Nightjars to begin their peculiar 'churring' calls.

There's plenty to see by walking the many paths that criss-cross around this area of forest. Several different habitats can be found, especially with the large heath area as well. There are Heathers, Sedges, Rushes and Grasses, as well as Ferns. Flowers number over 55 species and a large number of different Mosses as well. There are plenty of Fungi to be found too. A variety of Mammals live there: Roe, Fallow and Muntjac Deer, Badger, Rabbit, Stoat and Weasel, Voles, Shrews, several species of Mice, Mole and the Fox. About half of the UK Butterfly species and a very large number of Moths can be found there. You wouldn't be disappointed with the large number of Bird species throughout the year as well.

There are a great variety of trees, but one most noteworthy locally is named the 'Sun Oak', which is a very large old Oak which may be seen from the road in Hammerpond Lane.

ADDITIONAL PLACES WORTH A VISIT:
A bit further out from Horsham

FERRING BEACH AND ENVIRONS
BURTON MILL POND, NR PETWORTH
LOXWOOD CANAL AREA

FERRING BEACH AND ENVIRONS

Even here there are some plants to see as well as some sea waders and other Birds. The beach is shingle mostly except when tide is low revealing plenty of sand and rockpools in places. Also, at the top of the beach, there are marine environment plants such as Sea Holly, Sea Kale, Sea Bindweed, Toadflax, and the Dwarf Mallow which has a prostrate habit. Some butterflies may be seen on the coast, too, including the Clouded Yellow, which was my first sighting of it here.

Image 119 Dwarf Mallow on Ferring Beach. Photo July 2016

BURTON MILL POND, Nr Petworth
(Sussex)

Image 120   Common Sandpipers on a perch over the pond on a February day

This pond supports diverse wildlife and there are wooded walks also beyond the pond area where some really old trees with interesting trunks may be seen. I have enjoyed drawing many of these trees with pen and ink. During a visit there I saw some Common Sandpipers and a Swan on the pond. There are several wildfowl there and I am told that a Bittern may be present at dusk. There is also a 3.5mile circular trail taking in a small Nature Reserve and the Chingford Pond. The Burton Mill Pond is about 3 miles south of Petworth.

LOXWOOD CANAL AREA

This canal is part of the Wey & Arun Canal, and can be accessed in several locations. I prefer to start from the Onslow Arms Pub car park and walk along the towpath. One spring day when I walked with my family, there were many cowslips along the side of the canal. Some bees were very active outside a derelict building near the old mill.

Image 121   Cowslips by the Loxwood Canal, May 2015

Walking on a summer's day with a natural history group, there were many plants and wildflowers to be found. Purple Loosestrife, Vetch, Cowslips, Willowherbs, the invasive Balsam, and rather too much Giant Hogweed to name but a few.

Image 122　Bees by the old mill Loxwood. Photo May 2015

APPENDIX 1
ROOKWOOD NEWS
UPDATE 2020/2021

In the last few years, Horsham District Council (HDC) proposed to remove the Rookwood Green Space and golf course in favour of building about 1000 houses. It became apparent that many people as well as wildlife make use of the Rookwood area which spans North and South of the main road (Warnham Road) from the Robin Hood roundabout to Horsham North Parade, (which is on the way to the town). Any development, particularly North, would adversely impact the Nature Reserve. In fact, it would be catastrophic for the Nature Reserve! The wildlife also uses the Rookwood area as a corridor to the Reserve and if there was housing up to the Reserve boundaries many domestic pets, cats in particular, would prey on birds drastically, and numbers would decrease rapidly, spoiling the attraction of the Reserve. Also, noise, caused by humans so close by would impact on the serenity and safety of the wildlife on the Reserve. HDC have already increased the population of Horsham by thousands with massive housing estates, including the Wickhurst Green area as well as the 'work-in-progress' North Horsham site with around 2,500 homes. There is no reason, in my opinion, why they should entertain using Green Spaces for any further increase in the housing numbers. That would bring in loads more people, but reduce the number of Green Spaces that people would need and wish to use in their leisure time.

A timetable for submitting and acting on the housing proposals was drawn up by the Council. After petitions and an uproar of protests, a revised second plan was submitted (early 2021). This new plan suggested extending the Nature Reserve on the North side of the road, but with new houses to the South, but leaving the areas around Boldings Brook and the Red River. Probably, the old golf course lake area would then be surrounded by houses.

Following on from all the above, in late March 2021, it was reported in the local paper that all local objections have said an emphatic 'NO' to this project and asked for Rookwood to be removed from the possible housing sites list. Many local Groups and Neighbourhood Councils, including the Horsham Society, Keep-Rookwood-Green Alliance, Friends of the Warnham Local Nature Reserve, Rookwood Seniors Golf Society, Cootes Farm Community and the Horsham Town Community Partnership had all made their views known to HDC.

Later on in the WSCT Thursday 8th July 2021, it was reported that the unpopular plans to build new homes on Rookwood site had been withdrawn by the HDC. This was great news for everyone who objected to the plans and to all the local Groups who made a strong case for wildlife and public health reasons to keep this great site for everyone's use and how housing would destroy so much wonderful Green Space now needed more than ever in the North Horsham area. The Council have also said that it is vital to engage with local groups and find out how we can best use the Council owned land at Rookwood, and that the Council is committed to listening and engaging over the next two years before making any longer-term commitments on the future of Rookwood.

As local residents, we shall have to wait and see in the next two years what the Council's intentions are with regard to the future of the Rookwood site.

To the readers: please note that the above is my personal view on this matter. Author.

APPENDIX 2

Since writing the text for Knepp, in the Times Newspaper on 1st October 2022 was an article that Beavers are now recognised as a native species in the UK. This means that they may well be reintroduced to suitable sites across the country.

ANOTHER THREAT TO THE SUCCESS OF THE KNEPP PROJECT

In the WSCT 8th July 2021, alongside the reprieve for the Rookwood Green Space was a heading on four new strategic housing allocations that have been put forward: notably including 3,000 homes at Bucks Barn. Bucks Barn is a huge area that abuts on to the Knepp Estate. How disastrous would that be for the Wilding Project that has seen so much success in the last 20 years and where wildlife has found a safe environment and good habitat to re-establish? Many endangered species such as the Turtle Dove, Storks, and so on....

For the moment, the above plan has also been halted. I believe, the main reason now is that there is generally a water shortage in this whole area. This means no more large housing sites can be actioned until it can be shown to not add to the need for more water use from our rivers, and the Sussex reservoir.

To the readers: please note that the above is my personal view on this matter. Author.

LIST OF THE
AUTHOR'S PAINTINGS

a) Familiar Butterflies 1
b) Familiar Butterflies 2
c) Purple Fungi
d) Kestrel
e) Puffins
f) Red Fox
g) Fox sunning itself
h) Lapwings
i) Goosander
j) Odd-Bod, Magpie & Jackdaw
k) Sketch : Sparrowhawk and prey
l) Kingfisher
m) Grey Wagtail
n) Elder Berries and Blackberries
o) Tree 1 at Burton Mill Pond
p) Tree 2 at Burton Mill Pond
q) Elephant Hawk Moth & Hummingbird Hawk Moth
r) Greylag Goose

a) Familiar Butterflies 1

Top Left clockwise: Small Tortoiseshell, Peacock, Holly Blue, Orange-tip, Common Blue, Brimstone and Orange-tip

b) Familiar Butterflies 2

Top Left clockwise: Meadow Brown (m), Silver-washed Fritillary, Meadow Brown (f), Speckled Wood, Gatekeeper, Red Admiral, Painted Lady, Marbled White, Comma (closed wings), and Comma

c) Purple Fungi

d) Kestrel

e)   Puffins

f) Red Fox Sketch

g) Fox sunning itself

h) Lapwings

i) Goosander

j) Odd-Bod with Magpie and Jackdaw (Below)

k) Sketch: Sparrowhawk and prey

l) Kingfisher (Below)

m) Grey Wagtail

n) Elder Berries and Blackberries

o)   Tree 1: Burton Mill Pond

p)   Tree 2 Burton Mill Pond

q) Elephant Hawk Moth & Caterpillar (Left)
   Hummingbird Hawk Moth & Caterpillar (Right)

r)   Greylag Goose

ORGANISATIONS & TRUSTS OF NATURAL HISTORY INTEREST

Sussex Wildlife Trust
Woods Mill
Shoreham Road
Henfield
BN5 9SD

sussexwildlifetrust.org.uk

Warnham Local Nature Reserve
Warnham Road
Horsham
West Sussex RH12 2RA

warnhamnaturereservefriends.org.uk
or through: horsham.gov.uk/parks-and-countryside

Chesworth Farm
Chesworth Lane
Horsham
West Sussex RH13 0AA

friendsofchesworthfarm.com
or through: horsham.gov.uk/parks-and-countryside
Also Horsham's Green Spaces : horsham.gov.uk/parks-and-countryside

Knepp Estate
Small Dole
West Grinstead
RH13 8LJ

kneppestate.co.uk

Horsham Museum
9 The Causeways
Horsham
West Sussex RH12 1HE

horshammuseum.org

RSPB
The Lodge
Potton Road
Sandy
Bedfordshire SG19 2DL

rspb.org.uk

SUGGESTED OTHER BOOKS TO READ

Wilding, *The return of Nature to a British farm*	IsabellaTree	Picador
Extraordinary Insects *Weird. Wonderful. Indispensable. The Ones who run our World*	Anne Sverdrup-Thygeson	Mudlark
Say Goodbye to the Cuckoo	Michael McCarthy	John Murray Publishers
A Buzz in the Meadow	Dave Coulson	Vintage Books
The Secret Lives of Garden Birds *Including Illustrations and Photographs.*	Dominic Couzens	Helm/A & C Black publishers
The Butterflies of Sussex	Michael Blencowe & Neil Hulme	Pisces Publications

SOURCES AND REFERENCES

Collins Guide to Insects	Michael Chinery	William Collins
Collins Guide to British Wildlife	Paul Sterry	Harper Collins Publishers
Collins Complete Guide to British Butterflies & Moths	Paul Sterry, Andrew Cleave and Rob Read	William Collins
A Field Guide to Caterpillars of Butterflies & Moths	D J Carter & B Hargreaves	William Collins
Collins complete guide to British Mushrooms & Toadstools	Paul Sterry & Barry Hughes	Harper Collins
RSPB Ladybirds	Richard Comont	Bloomsbury Wildlife
RSPB Bumblebees	Richard Comont	Bloomsbury Wildlife
RSPB spotlight Foxes	Mike Unwin	Bloomsbury Natural History
Wild Flowers of Britain & Ireland	Marjorie Blamey, Richard Fitter & Alastair Fitter	Bloomsbury Publishing

Bird (illustrated Guide to Birds Of Britain & Europe)	Peter Hayman & Rob Hume	Mitchell Beazley
Birds of Sussex	Sussex Ornithology Society	BTO Books
Wilding	Isabella Tree	Picador
Mammals of Britain Their Tracks, Trails & Signs	M J Lawrence & R W Brown	Blandford Press

ABOUT THE AUTHOR

Heather grew up in the Surrey countryside showing an interest in natural history from her early childhood. She was always keen to learn the names of birds, butterflies and wild flowers found in the fields and hedgerows near her home. After a busy family life, and now retired in Horsham, Heather spends some of her time looking out for interesting natural history subjects to draw and paint as well as increasing her knowledge of them. She is also a local artist, and keen gardener.

Previous Book: *A Celebration of Flowers* (from the Horsham Museum Garden) 2012